What a tremendous resource this  *The Field" is a thoroughly unique and i_____. I am certain that it will be used as a m_____ ... Bible-centered churches. The uniqueness of this book is found in its thorough, in-depth Bible study on the matter of one discerning God's plan for his life. Yet it doesn't stop with simply the discernment of God's will; it takes you on the journey of discovering the joys and utter benefits of fulfilling God's plan for your life. It will also serve as a tool to encourage one to simply stay faithful to accomplish God's plan when times get turbulent and it appears that not much fruit is being borne in your personal field. I am constantly on the lookout for good books for thoughtful students about the issues of Christian living. "Buy The Field" is one I can whole-heartedly recommend for any serious disciple of Christ.*

~Morris Gleiser, Evangelist, Indianapolis, IN and Author, *The Journey: Navigating your Teenage Years.*

A successful life, versus a life of disappointment and failure can be determined by finding the will of God for one's life and doing it. Rob Fleshman has written an excellent book on this subject that is a pleasure to read, as his manuscript contrasts the Biblical view of a life and the secular approach to it. If everyone in our city or town knew, believed, and lived according to the truths of this writing, we would have a sanctuary.

~Dr. Tom Wallace, Evangelist and Pastor Emeritus of Franklin Road Baptist Church in Murfeesboro, TN

Finding your field! As a pastor at the same church for a long time, I have seen the frustration in fellow Christians' lives as they struggle to find their cause or place in the work of God. In this book, Pastor Fleshman does a phenomenal job of helping everyone to see that there is a field just for you and that God has you picked out for such a field! I strongly endorse this book! Read it, live it, and Buy Your Field!

~Dr. Randy Dignan, Pastor of Bible Baptist Church in Jefferson City, MO, home to Listening Heart Ministries.

I am thankful for the resolve of Pastor Fleshman to write a book that can be of practical help to our Independent Baptist Churches. I appreciate the insight that "Buy the Field" offers into Bible truth and Rob Fleshman's ability to illustrate, making it easier for the reader to make application. You will be confronted with the reality that God has a definite plan for your life and convicted by His requirement of stewardship over this life, yet at the same time encouraged by the powerful provision that God has made available!

~ Billy Ingram, Evangelist

Reading a spiritual book should inspire change and cause one to stand in awe at the greatness of God and the clear teaching He has delivered through His word. Pastor Fleshman has done this by focusing on a very consuming subject for every believer. If one doesn't find and follow God's purpose for life then they have missed what life is all about! The uniquely interwoven illustration of "Buying the field" is a masterful and meaningful way of portraying this powerful truth. The personal touch and thought provoking material of both biblical and illustrated truth is a perfect blend. Rob's writing style is easy and pleasing to read and deeply focused on the heart. This book will no doubt challenge you, convict and correct you, comfort you and change you to pursue the most profitable existence you can have. If you are seeking to grow in Christ and to walk in the "good and acceptable and perfect will of God" then "Buy the Field" is a must read!

~Mike Herbster, Evangelist and Director of Southland Christian Camp in Ringgold, Louisiana

BUY THE FIELD

Find, Follow and Finish God's Call for Your Life

Rob Fleshman

WESTBOW
PRESS
A DIVISION OF THOMAS NELSON

WestBow Press books may be ordered through booksellers or by contacting:

WestBow Press
A Division of Thomas Nelson
1663 Liberty Drive
Bloomington, IN 47403
www.westbowpress.com
1-(866) 928-1240

ISBN: 978-1-4497-9294-7 (sc)
ISBN: 978-1-4497-9293-0 (hc)
ISBN: 978-1-4497-9295-4 (e)

Library of Congress Control Number: 2013907725

Printed in the United States of America.

WestBow Press rev. date: 5/3/2013

The author wishes to sincerely thank Tony Valentine for his unwavering efforts and assistance in providing editing services for the manuscript.

This book is dedicated to the love of my life, Michelle. Who, for more than twenty years of marriage, has never yielded to any such temptation to quit or turn back on the field of marriage she bought on a cold winter's day in December of 1991.

Thank you for being a faithful source of inspiration and courage for me, our four children, and all those who long to find, follow, and finish God's call for their life.

CONTENTS

PREFACE

Again, the kingdom of heaven is like unto treasure hid in a field; the which when a man hath found, he hideth, and for joy thereof goeth and selleth all that he hath, and buyeth that field. (Matthew 13:44)

Hundreds of artists have etched onto canvas enduring, picturesque images of their favorite sort. Musicians have sung of the strawberry variety. Developers' build on them, lovers go for long strolls in them, farmers intensively labor in them and realtors do their level best to buy and sell them. Whatever part of the country one calls home, from baseball to cotton, wheat to soccer, and football to pumpkins, we are inescapably surrounded by fields.

But despite sharing a common name, this book concerns itself with none of such fields. Rather it has as its lofty aim to arrest the consciousness, raise the awareness, whet the appetite and prayerfully, serve as a call to action for the finding, following and finishing of your calling: your field. I am referring to that acutely personal, high calling of God and vocational pursuit that is part and parcel of His plan for the lives of every one of His children. Perhaps for you it is the CONSTRUCTION field. For another it is the EDUCATION field. For still others it may well be the NURSING field, MECHANICS field, YOUTH MINISTRY FIELD, the CULINARY ARTS field or hundreds of other such fields that could be cited. Whatever your God-appointed field, may the biblical precepts presented in the following pages ever serve to inspire you to buy the field, to work your field, and to stay in that same field for the cause of Christ.

INTRODUCTION

*I*n the months leading up to the 2008 Presidential elections in the United States, then Governor of Alaska, and hopeful Republican Presidential Nominee, Sarah Palin was repeatedly questioned about her support for a project in her state that had come to be known as "The Bridge to Nowhere". The rationale behind the proposed construction of this bridge was to bring together Gravina Island and the town of Ketchikan, Alaska. With no paved roads, restaurants, or stores of any kind, and touting a whopping populous of 50 residents, Gravina Island seemed the most unlikely of all destinations for the construction of a bridge which blueprints called to be 80 feet taller than New York's famed Brooklyn Bridge and nearly as long as San Francisco's photogenic Golden Gate Bridge.

The "nail in the coffin" to these well laid plans came in the form of public awareness and much negative press that surrounded the projected cost of the publicly funded bridge, $398 million. Or roughly $8 million per island resident. The Gravina Island bridge project increasingly became viewed as a poster-child tribute to pork barrel spending, prompting Governor Palin to eventually retract her previous support for the initiative. Congress likewise promptly de-funded the $223 million that they had earmarked for the now doomed bridge to nowhere land.

The Original Bridge to Nowhere

The Gravina Island Bridge may well be the most highly publicized bridge of recent memory never to have been built on U.S. soil, but it was by no means the first proposed bridge to nowhere. In the 1970's, construction was underway on the Olimpijka, a planned east-west three-hundred and ten mile long motorway across the country of Poland that linked highway infrastructure between Berlin and Moscow. While originally expected to open in time for the 1980 summer Olympic Games held in Moscow, gripping economic times would ensue Poland, as well as a tumultuous political landscape and ever shifting national priorities. All of this led up to the construction being halted and the eventual abandonment of the entire Olimpijka project.

The culmination of all of the planning and time and effort was that a single 31 mile section between Wrzesnia and Konin was completed and opened for use in the 1980's. In the final analysis, though, only 10%, a tithe if you will, of the 310 mile long dream came to fruition. The remainder of what was realized from Olimpijka construction is a vagabond collection of ruins. A field lined with 40-50 concrete support pillars thrusting high into the Polish sky, intended to undergird the highway, but now stands isolated with only the nests of birds to support on its sturdy frame. A meadow lined with trees all cleared in vain. Piles of dirt here, a graffiti stained aqueduct there, and a most curious ~loo foot long isolated section of a concrete viaduct proudly resting on pillars jutting some 30 feet in the air. Apparently, plans were for it to be an overpass when it grew up, but alas it passes over nothing but scrub brush and the scrapped plans of men. The stand-alone structure comes from out of nowhere and serves as a bridge to nowhere as well.

Taking all of this vanquished scenery in, the 100% planned but 90% unfinished Olimpijka bears a striking resemblance to the modern day dreams and life pursuits of so many Christians. Such carefully wished upon plans, but in the end never having really materialized and leaving behind fragments of ruin as a testimony to what might have been. Chalk it up to a myriad of causes; a financial crunch, a failed relationship, raising a family, a bad health report from the doctor or even a mid-life crisis that starts long before and runs well past mid-life. The excuses are all too numerous and the end results all too predictable: Olimpijka.

It has been estimated that in Bible times, the Israelites stepped out in faith and conquered only about 10% of the land that God had in store for His people. That's about the same percentage as what project Olimpijka managed to check off as "done" in the 1980's, and 10% is probably dangerously close to that which the average Christian today realizes of all the plans that God has in store for us.

Incidentally, it turns out that the forever to remain unfinished Olimpijka roadway was slated to be built over much of a planned, but also unfinished, east-west motorway that Nazi Germany began construction on after their invasion of Poland. And as another proof point of history often times repeating itself, after much planning, construction was initiated on the A2 motorway in 2010. The blueprints for this latest rendition of the east-west highway calls for it to be built right over the top of (you guessed it) what would have been Olimpijka. Any and all remnants of Olimpijka are scheduled to be torn down and destroyed as part of construction of the A2.

Better pick up the pace and blow the dust off your well-intended plans, and the blueprints of your life's dream. The heavy earth moving equipment of time and neglect are seen rolling in from the distance and the bulldozers of regret and missed opportunities are about to fire up their engines.

PART I

Finding God's Call

Believe with all of your heart that you will do what you were made to do.
~Orison Swett Marden

Decision and determination are the engineer and
fireman of our train to opportunity and success.
~Burt Lawlor

In a free society, every opportunity comes with three obligations. First,
you must seize it. You must mold it into a work that brings value to
others. Second, you must live it. Opportunity is nurtured only by action.
Third, you must defend the freedom to pursue opportunities . . .
~Robert C. Goizueta

Twenty years from now you will be more disappointed by the
things you didn't do than by the ones you did do. So throw
off the bowlines. Sail away from the safe harbor. Catch the
trade winds in your sails. Explore. Dream. Discover.
~Mark Twain

CHAPTER #1

You Have a Field

Let thine eyes be on the field . . . (Ruth 2:9)

The opening verse of a favorite children's song sung in Sunday Schools and Vacation Bible Schools across this country is as follows,

O, be careful little eyes what you see. O, be careful little eyes what you see. For the Father up above is looking down in love, so be careful little eyes what you see.

The balance of this short melody's verses offer up the same cautionary challenge to one's ears, tongue, mind, hands and feet. The emphasis is on the tongue not saying wrong things or the feet not going to wrong places, and so forth. Doing, speaking, hearing, thinking, going and seeing things which they ought not would fall under the unenviable banner of sins of commission. That is, committing those acts of sin which are contrary to the teachings of scripture.

But there is another manner of sin. It is every bit equally offensive to a Holy God and yet routinely flies well below the radar in the life of the busy Christian. I am referring not to the committing of wrong things, but rather to the omitting of right things. *Therefore to him that knoweth to do good, and doeth it not, to him it is sin.* (James 4:17) These good deeds left altogether undone are classified as sins of omission. Equally repugnant, but receiving far less press, these iniquities are when we unwisely leave undone the doing, saying or thinking of right things which we know ought to be done, said or meditated upon.

> *Finally, brethren, whatsoever things are true, whatsoever things are honest, whatsoever things are just, whatsoever things are pure, whatsoever things are lovely, whatsoever things are of good report; if there be any virtue, and if there be any praise, think on these things. ⁹ Those things, which ye have both learned, and received, and heard, and seen in me, do: and the God of peace shall be with you.* (Philippians 4:8-9)

Pure things such as sharing the gospel with others; just things like giving our best to God; and true things such as letting our mind's eye be on the field, as the writer of the book of Ruth admonishes. *Let thine eyes be on the field that they do reap, and go thou after them:* (Ruth 2:9) Ruth needed the basic sustenance of food and water. Boaz was aware of Ruth's predicament and had provisions in place for meeting her every need and so much more. But for those provisions to journey from his hand to hers, the initial instruction for Ruth to obey was to . . . *let thine eyes be on the field.* The reason being was that Boaz, the Kinsman Redeemer and a type of the Lord Jesus Christ, not only had a plan to meet her need; he also had a place. The place was a specific field where that plan was to be fulfilled. If Ruth's eyes were affixed anywhere other than the field she was directed towards, then the plan would not be accomplished, at least not as God had intended, and she would unnecessarily lack and suffer.

EARS, OPEN. EYEBALLS, CLICK.

Whether we give credence to the notion or not, children are protégés, apprentices to life, in more ways than adults often take the time to consider. God has implanted within fashionable young minds a great capacity to learn and such learning is best assimilated through modeling the mannerisms of their mentors, including parents, teachers, pastors and other authority figures in their lives. However, this assimilation of learning through mentorship is a two-edged sword. While helpful traits that serve to enable await their inheritance, so do hindering habits which exist only to cripple.

One such crippling habit is a lack of godly aim and focus. A life marked by great achievement for God is the byproduct of a life of great focus and singularity to please the Lord. Paul knew the unbridled power of a Christ-focused, surrendered life when, under the inspiration of the Holy Spirit, he penned these words.

> A life marked by great achievement for God is the byproduct of a life of great focus and singularity to please the Lord.

> *Brethren, I count not myself to have apprehended: but this one thing I do, forgetting those things which are behind, and reaching forth unto those things which are before, I press toward the mark for the prize of the high calling of God in Christ Jesus.* (Philippians 3:13-14)

Knowing this as well, Satan is relentless in his base work of distraction and untiring in his sinister attempts to keep the eyes of Christians off of God and out of focus with His will for their lives. In such times, we unwittingly yield to subtle temptations again and again. What is the biblical antidote when we find ourselves entrenched in the abysmal mire of a clouded, distracted life? Simply this: purposeful, highly intentional living powered by focus. Concerning focus in the area of business success, J. Paul Getty once said:

The individual who wants to reach the top in business must appreciate the might of the force of habit-and must understand that practices are what create habits. He must be quick to break those habits that can break him-and hasten to adopt those practices that will become the habits that help him achieve the success he desires.

One exercise for teachers within the realm of children's ministry for regaining the lost attention and focus of their pupils is, "Ears-Open! Eyeballs-Click!" (I am told that it also a tried and true tool for Marine Corps drill instructors) When children's minds are in a vagabond state of meandering and inattention, the teacher may shout out, "EARS!" The response expected from the class is, "OPEN!" To which the teacher again shouts, "EYEBALLS!" And the expected reply from the children is "CLICK!" By declaring "ears" and "eyeballs," the teacher is wooing dull-of-hearing ears and distracted eyes to meander no longer. By responding in unison with "open" and "click," the students acknowledge that their attention and vision has been diverted to lesser, trivial pursuits as they resolve to re-focus their focus.

Sitting still and attentively listening in a Sunday school classroom may feel like an eternity at times to a fidgety seven year old, but we would all agree that it is most definitely not. Resolving to be focused over the span of forty-five or sixty *minutes* in the class room is admirable, but how does one stay focused on God's call for their life over the span of forty-five or even sixty *years?*

PHOROPTERS AND THE WORD OF GOD

Phoropter. Just reading the word and sounding it through may conjure up some diverse imagery in our mind's eye. Is it a lesser known, distant cousin twice removed of the Velociraptor? No and grab your parka and track down some mittens stat because you are freezing cold. Is it one of the umpteen stainless dental instruments that your dentist asks for once you have nestled down in the chair sporting a stylish clip-on bib? No, but to give credit where it is due, you are far less frigid than just a few moments ago and it is probably safe to take off the mittens and trade the parka in for a light windbreaker.

A phoropter is an instrument that most of us at one time or another have placed our foreheads against and looked through while sitting in the seat at the eye doctor's office. However precise we imagined our vision to be when we entered the place, the true health and condition of our eye sight is brought to light via this instrument. We may have fancied ourselves to have 20/20 vision or even better, but the phoropter is unbiased and is not influenced by our confident swagger as we smugly plop ourselves down in the chair. When in use by one trained such as an Optometrist, there is no guesswork needed as to the condition of our eye sight. Over the course of the next few minutes, however in or out of focus our eyes are, will be made unmistakably clear.

God has His spiritual phoropter as well: however, you don't have to use spell checker to write it or hunt down a dictionary for the correct pronunciation. God's phoropter is called the Bible and it is the primary means for Christians to stay focused as we make our way through this sin-marred world.

> *For the word of God is quick, and powerful, and sharper than any twoedged sword, piercing even to the dividing asunder of soul and spirit, and of the joints and marrow, and is a discerner of the thoughts and intents of the heart. Neither is there any creature that is not manifest in his sight: but all things are naked and opened unto the eyes of him with whom we have to do.* (Hebrews 4:12-13)

The writer of the book of James provides another layer of perspective with these words.

> *But be ye doers of the word, and not hearers only, deceiving your own selves. For if any be a hearer of the word, and not a doer, he is like unto a man beholding his natural face in a glass: For he beholdeth himself, and goeth his way, and straightway forgetteth what manner of man he was. But whoso looketh into the perfect law of liberty, and continueth therein, he being not a forgetful hearer, but a doer of the work, this man shall be blessed in his deed.* (James 1:22-25)

While Optometrists generally advise us to schedule annual times behind the phoropter, the Great Physician would have the Christian to place himself under His phoropter daily. Psalm 88:9 instructs, *Mine eye mourneth by reason of affliction: LORD, I have called daily upon thee,* and the Bereans are commended for their time each day in the Word of God, *These were more noble than those in Thessalonica, in that they received the word with all readiness of mind, and searched the scriptures daily, whether those things were so.* (Acts 17:11)

As an Optometrist is mindful that our fleshly eyesight is ever failing, God knows that our spiritual eyesight is likewise prone to falter and in continual need of re-focus. And so in loving kindness, He made provision for just that by giving us His eternal, unfailing Word. God instructs the lukewarm, self-satisfied church of Laodicea, *I counsel thee to . . . anoint thine eyes with eyesalve, that thou mayest see.* (Revelation 3:18) That cleansing, vision restoring balm which re-focuses our focus and washes away the dirt, grime and unprofitable distractions from our eyes was, is and always will be the pure Word of God. *That he might sanctify and cleanse it with the washing of water by the word,* (Ephesians 5:26) and, *Now ye are clean through the word which I have spoken unto you.* (John 15:3)

What a timeless lesson to be learned for the soul fatigued by years of living a distracted life, void of its God-called purpose! What a needful reminder to the Christian going through the vain motions of day-to-day life distinctly lacking the Christ-honoring focus God desires for each of His children.

WHAT'S YOUR SPIRITUAL PSI?

Not long ago, I was in the market for a pressure washer to use occasionally around our home. I made my way over to the local hardware store where I was not disappointed in the impressive line-up of models to choose from. Everything from an ultra-light apparatus wand that attaches to the end of a garden hose, all the way up to a beastly machine powered by a bone-jarring nineteen horsepower engine, packing a massive 5,000 PSI (pounds per square inch) and capable of unleashing 5 GPM (gallons per minute). I stood in awe as my mind ran rampant with thoughts such as:

> *How on earth have I been able to live life up to this point without this puppy in my possession?*
>
> *How much would it set me back to add a 3rd car garage onto our house so that we can have a place to park this metal monstrosity, weighing in about as much as a heifer?*
>
> *In the hands of a novice, would this device meet the criteria set forth by the military to be classified as a WMD (Weapon of Mass Destruction)?*
>
> *Is purchasing this machine sort of like buying a firearm for hunting, in that I have to be registered and go through a pressure washer safety course and wear an orange vest and cap when I use it?*

A salesperson walked over and handed me a paper towel to wipe the drool from my mouth that was trickling down my chin and had begun to form a puddle on the floor below. As he plopped down the "Caution: Wet Floors" yellow signage beside me, he began to dote about what this thing would do. I listened in earnest and midway through the spiel, I inquired as to why there were five different colored tips; one each of white, black, green, yellow and red? He explained the white one was for dispensing soap through the machine and that black was for general use such as washing a car, while green was for jobs like removing grime off a wooden deck or removing old paint from a fence. I inquired of him as to what the yellow one was used for? Initially he did not have much of a response, except to say that perhaps it could be used to remove fresh paint off of metal-sort of a wet form of sand-blasting. In the area that we were living in at the time, nearly everyone in the subdivision had 1x4 treated lumber fencing around their yard, and he made mention that the intensity of the pressure would simply split the boards in two.

My eyebrows perked up in a northerly direction, as an outward tell-tale sign of the approval that had already taken place inwardly in my heart. I was thoroughly impressed. This was love at first sight. Clearly this was the machine that I was being led to purchase for such a time as this. But one question remained. "What about the red tip? What's that one used for?" I inquired. Some things are just better left unsaid and this final portion of our discussion would probably fall into that category. His countenance changed from one of exuberance as he rattled on about the many attributes of this beastly machine to that of soberness. I sensed a hesitance in his voice that was not present before. No legal, consumer-safe uses for the red tip could be readily cited. Perhaps it was an embellishment, a bit of salesman one-upmanship, or maybe there was an element of truth in the next words that were spoken. Essentially he said that if you were to use the red tip while power washing without wearing any shoes, that should you aim it down at your foot, it would cut your toes clean off.

Whoa, there Nelly! As accident prone as I can be, I knew that no machine, even one as beautifully destructive as this one, was worth losing a bodily extremity over. So, I came back down to earth, lowered my expectations while swallowing my pride and purchased the 2500 PSI model. I am proud to say that I still have all ten toes safely intact. For now.

But what made the difference between the white and the red tip? Why was the white tip safe to use on anything, while the red tip could have been housed behind glass with stenciled letters that read, "Use only in case of emergency?" In a word, it is what we have been talking about much of this first chapter: focus. The white, black, green, yellow, and red tips were colored as such, because the orifice where the water flowed out of was much larger on the white and black tips. But on the yellow and red tips, the opening was much smaller, greatly constricting the water and dispensing it with much more focused, restricted intensity.

And so it is in the Christian's life. Every Christian is connected to and powered by the Holy Spirit of God, *But ye have an unction from the Holy One . . .* (1 John 2:20a) The difference is some "white-tipped" Christians go through the motions of everyday life distracted, lacking in focused direction and purpose, rendering them largely powerless to do much that matters for God and counts for eternity. And then there are those ultra-focused, highly intentional "red-tipped" Christians. Men and women who live their life in view of a call and have the power of God upon them to make a difference in impacting their families and the world around them for the cause of Christ. Of course between those two extremes reside black, green, and yellow-tipped Christians as well, each life demonstrating various levels of "spiritual PSI".

Hey, what "color" of a Christian are you? Almost certainly the most well-known and beloved children's song of all-time is, "Jesus Loves Me." One part of the chorus is, *Red, brown, yellow, black and white; they are precious in His sight. Jesus loves the little children of the world.* In line with our personal spiritual PSI assessment, we could tweak the lyrics to, *Red, green, yellow, black and white, all tips are precious in His sight. Jesus loves the many Christians of the world.* Regardless of what color your tip, Jesus loves you; make no mistake of that. However, I am of the persuasion that it is the "red tip" and "yellow tip" genre of Christians who Jesus is the most precious to. These are the Christians who most often demonstrate their love for Jesus and seem to be the most passionate about finding His call upon their life.

MODERN DAY LOTUS EATERS

Within the realm of Greek mythology, the lotus-eaters were a race of people from an island near North Africa dominated by lotus plants. The lotus fruits and flowers were the primary food of the island and a highly addictive narcotic, lulling the people to sleep in peaceful apathy, entirely removed of all care and concern for their surroundings. As a result, they soon became pleasure addicts-unwittingly enslaved to the intoxicating lure of the lotus flower.

In *Odyssey IX*, Odysseus describes how while he and his men were headed west to Ithaca, strong averse northerly winds blew them off their sailing course.

> *I was driven thence by foul winds for a space of nine days upon the sea, but on the tenth day we reached the land of the Lotus-eaters, who live on a food that comes from a kind of flower. Here we landed to take in fresh water, and our crews got their mid-day meal on the shore near the ships.*

> *When they had eaten and drunk I sent two of my company to see what manner of men the people of the place might be, and they had a third man under them. They started at once, and went about among the Lotus-Eaters, who did them no hurt, but gave them to eat of the lotus, which was so delicious that those who ate of it left off caring about home, and did not even want to go back and say what had happened to them, but were for staying and munching lotus with the Lotus-eaters without thinking further of their return; nevertheless, though they wept bitterly I forced them back to the ships and made them fast under the benches. Then I told the rest to go on board at once, lest any of them should taste of the lotus and leave off wanting to get home, so they took their places and smote the grey sea with their oars.*[1]

Odysseus and his men were on a noble quest en route to Ithaca. There was guided purpose. There was clear direction. There was intentional pursuit. They were a mission-minded band of brothers out on the high seas adventure of their lifetime. But they encountered tremendous adversity in the form of a streak of nine days of unrelenting northerly winds, resulting in being blown completely off course and dropping anchor in a land where they ought not to have. They pulled up a chair, sat down and kicked their feet up on the ottoman amongst a room chock full of human sloths. The Bible has much to say about the kind of road-trip buddies that we should (and should not) keep.

> *Blessed is the man that walketh not in the counsel of the ungodly, nor standeth in the way of sinners, nor sitteth in the seat of the scornful.* (Psalm 1:1)

> *Be not deceived: evil communications corrupt good manners.* (1 Corinthians 15:33)

> *But Amnon had a friend.* (2 Samuel 13:3)

Aimlessly off course in their direction, and hopelessly off task in their thinking, the men lowered something far more precious than their anchor that day-they lowered their guard. Hmmm, ever been there, done that? Your walk with Christ is sweet. Your steps are guided. Your thought life is pure. Your joy is overflowing. Your way is blessed. Then, in an unsuspecting moment, a foul northerly blows into your life. Perhaps you fight against it for a season, perhaps longer. Perhaps not even at all. Whatever the case, the end result is usually the same, as your life drifts off course. Way off course. In golf vernacular, you are so OB (out of bounds). Penalty strokes are assessed. An awkward hush settles upon the watching gallery. The cameras are live streaming your play by awful play. Things turn ugly as they always do when our once affixed eyes begin to wonder and when the wooing of temptation to stray reaches a fever pitch; we cave. Again.

Fortunately, Lotus-eaters solicited by the draw of selfish pleasure and sensual consumption are restricted to the corridors of Greek mythology. Unfortunately, their self-pleasing, apathetic pursuits do not know such mythical boundaries. Purposeless journeys are no respecter of geographical or demographical limits. Empty living is quite infinite in scope. The expanse of an unfocused life reaches to the uttermost. The extent of vain pursuits is, to quote legendary thinker Buzz Lightyear, "To infinity and beyond." Do not let your guard down to such trappings, as Odysseus' men did. A very non-fictional devil is burning the candle at both ends to blow Christian men, women, and young people off the God-orchestrated course for their life. He tirelessly attempts to keep their eyes blind and their minds oblivious to the field that God has for them.

The seeds of the addictive Lotus plants are nurtured and take root only in the rich soil of Odyssey fiction. But Satan has no such shortage of narcotic seeds which, without a God-driven focus, will delight to take root in the fertile soil of one's heart. To be shamelessly blunt: your heart. Three of the four gospels feature the story of the Parable of the Sower. In the account, the Sower broadcasts seeds, (symbolic of the Word of God) in four different soil settings, (symbolic of the human heart) each responding differently to the seeds. Satan is the great imitator and he too broadcasts his own hellish seed on a variety of human hearts as well. Oh, be careful little eyes what you see. *Let thine eyes be on the field.*

To give anything less than your best is to sacrifice the gift.
~Steve Prefontaine

It is better to wear out than to rust out.
~Bishop Richard Cumberland

You can't build a reputation on what you are going to do.
~Henry Ford

Opportunity knocks at the strangest times, It's not the time that matters But how you answer the door.
~Steve Gray

Chance is always powerful. Let your hook be always cast; in the pool where you least expect it, there will be a fish.

CHAPTER 2

The Field is Sacred

But the field . . . shall be holy unto the Lord; as a field devoted;
(Leviticus 27:21a)

*F*ollowers of Christ come in all shapes, sizes, colors, and yes, even in all vocational backgrounds. There are Christian lawyers, teachers, plumbers, athletes, bankers, nurses, sales managers, technicians, customer service representatives and entrepreneurs, to name but a few of the many fields. And there is nothing wrong with such vocations; in fact, there is everything good and right and even sacred with these and countless other endeavors IF those are the vocations God would have for us. But sooner or later, inevitable problems rear their dreaded heads when there is a gap between our chosen field and that field which divine Providence has chosen for us. It may come as a complete surprise, but the same God who by His spoken word commanded into existence every fabric of the entire universe has placed a personal calling from on High for every believer that is in Christ Jesus.

> *For I know the thoughts that I think toward you, saith the LORD,*
> *thoughts of peace, and not of evil, to give you an expected end.*
> (Jeremiah 29:11)

> *According as he hath chosen us in him before the foundation of the world, that we should be holy and without blame before him in love:* (Ephesians 1:4)

Wise is the Christian that lives in light of this truth and unreservedly seeks God's face for all decisions, small and great. We have assurance from the Bible that God is not elusive and will reveal His appointed direction for our lives to all who seek His will.

SECULAR MEET SACRED

We have a way of attempting to segregate the secular from the sacred. For many of us, we view our activities from 12:01 PM on Sunday (or until the final "amen" in the worship service, whichever should come first) to the prelude to worship the following Lord's Day morning as secular. In other words, sacred pursuits are wrongfully confined to worship services at church and perhaps time spent in private devotions at home. There are 168 hours over the course of seven days-Is one or two hours a week the sum total of our pursuit of sacred endeavors? I mean, does God's plan for His children consist of less than 2% of our time on this earth to be spent in sacred devotion and service to Him? If so, then secularism trumps, no it trounces, the sacred; relegating sacredness as largely inconsequential in the landscape of our daily lives.

But what if we were to turn such prevalent and unbiblical thinking upside down? Instead of viewing life as subdivided into all things secular and sacred in 2D on a thirteen inch black and white TV, (you know, the one some of us are old enough to have grown up with, which had a protruding rabbit ears antenna along with a mono speaker veiled behind a cheap plastic housing just below the rotary channel dial sporting thirteen, count 'em thirteen channels!) what if we looked upon all the events of daily life in more of a conglomerated fashion in 3D? We're talking high-definition plasma, baby. Seventy-two inches of flat screen,

HD heaven; packing more pixel density than you can shake a stick at. However iconoclastic, I contend such a mental convergence of the sacred and secular is foundational and biblical. And the end result of such a perspective finds the secular packing its bags, heading off to catch the red eye to a land far, far away on permanent furlough, leaving sacred as the last virtue standing.

Secular is a categorical term cleverly devised by man as a catch-all for everything not deemed sacred. And in such a flawed context as described on the previous page, pretty much everything would be deemed not sacred. Traditional thinking confines the notion of sacred to only a handful of activities that are explicitly religious. So then all of life's other grand experiences, as well as everyday occurrences, must be dubbed as secular. With this viewpoint having such an illegitimate stronghold on Christian thinking, it is no wonder that so many bow down and prostrate themselves to the awesome influence of the god of secularism. Sure, we offer streaky devotion now and then to Jesus Christ and to all things sacred-but our real god, at least the one we prefer to spend the most time with, resides ever so comfortably in the secular.

Take heart. We are not the inaugural generation guilty of saying one thing and doing another. This is not the first time in the course of human history where people's walk has been out of step with their talk. Nope, we come from a long, inglorious line of fence straddlers. Since the beginning of time, scores of folks have been known to talk the talk and yet fail to walk the walk, content to give lip service to God. It was so in Elijah's day, and even Jesus had to contend with it during His earthly ministry.

Ye hypocrites, well did Esaias prophesy of you, saying, This people draweth nigh unto me with their mouth, and honoureth me with their lips; but their heart is far from me. But in vain they do worship me, teaching for doctrines the commandments of men. (Matthew 15:7-9)

As someone has well stated, *Your talk talks and your walk talks; But your walk talks louder than your talk talks.* True, we are not the first generation of inconsistent Christians bent on living life smack dab in the middle of the road; but if our hearts would be resolved to simply obey the things of God and worship Him in spirit and in truth, our generation could be the one that breaks the cycle of inconsistency. This could be the time and we could be the people where the proverbial "buck" stops.

The argument for things we once thought of as secular being captive to the sacred is a persuasive one, and I am convinced that a convergence of the secular and sacred is God's vantage point on the whole matter as well. While we are inclined to erect mental pylons in an effort to ensure there are distinct designations between the two entities, the God who knows everything knows no such thing. Just to level-set our thinking, sacred could best be defined as holy or devoted; as in, *But the field . . . shall be holy unto the Lord; as a field devoted.* (Leviticus 27:21)

In this context, a field is nothing more than cultivated dirt. What on earth is so sacred about dirt? Outside of an impassioned agronomist looking for the next breakthrough in soil sciences, or an inventive six year old with his heart set on serving up some of his world famous mud pies, what is so bedazzling about soil? Perhaps to you and me, not much at all; but to the God who created everything (including dirt) for His enduring glory, all is sacred. *Thou art worthy, O Lord, to receive glory and honour and power: for thou hast created all things, and for thy pleasure they are and were created.* (Revelation 4:11) God has done some pretty amazing things with dirt before, *And the LORD God formed man of the dust of the ground, and breathed into his nostrils the breath of life; and man became a living soul.* (Genesis 2:7) As God breathes new life in and through His children, I am quite certain He is still able to do some amazing things with us today.

As a living soul created by God, whatever your life's calling, it is of a very sacred nature and it matters to God. Knowing this, we should give Him our very best in the workplace (and everyplace else). Martin Luther was noted as having once stated:

The maid who sweeps her kitchen is doing the will of God just as much as the clergy who prays—not because she may sing a Christian hymn as she sweeps but because God loves clean floors. The Christian shoemaker does his Christian duty not by putting little crosses on the shoes, but by making good shoes, because God is interested in good craftsmanship.[1]

God has a vested interest in how His children perform daily tasks at work, in the home, at school, and out in the community; even tasks that our culture has labeled as secular. Don't take my word for it; take His as you meditate on the following passages of scripture.

Whatsoever thy hand findeth to do, do it with thy might; for there is no work, nor device, nor knowledge, nor wisdom, in the grave, whither thou goest. (Ecclesiastes 9:10)

Whether therefore ye eat, or drink, or whatsoever ye do, do all to the glory of God. (1 Corinthians 10:31)

And whatsoever ye do, do it heartily, as to the Lord, and not unto men; Knowing that of the Lord ye shall receive the reward of the inheritance: for ye serve the Lord Christ. (Colossians 3:23-24)

HOLY GROUND AND SHOES THAT WALK ON IT

One of the great preachers from yesteryear, Harry Ironside, grew up in a home with his widowed mother, as his Dad died of typhoid when Harry was two. When he was not in school, Harry could be found down at the shoemaker shop, working for a cobbler, in order that he might help his mom make ends meet. Harry's employer, Dan Mackay, was a beam of Christian light to his community. He was a man who found Christ's call on his life and was living it for the glory of God.

In some respects, Mackay's tiny little shop could have passed for an aspiring chapel of sorts, as scripture was posted all along its humble walls. On the shop's front counter there was always a stack of gospel tracts nestled beside an open Bible. Inside every package which was couriered from that shop, a note containing scripture could be found, and rare was the patron that walked away from that humble storefront without being spoken to of their need for salvation in Christ and by faith in Him alone.

Young Harry's chief duties were to hammer the leather used for the sole of the shoe. The proper process for making long lasting shoe soles seems antiquated today, but a piece of leather would be cut to fit and then placed in a bucket of water to soak. Harry's job was to take the piece of leather and to pound it until it was completely dry. It would then be ready to be nailed to the shoe. As you can imagine, this process of hammering each sole took a long time and much effort on the part of the young lad, but he was assured by the owner that it was necessary.

Mackay was not the only cobbler in town (but perhaps the only honest one) as another shoe shop was along the route that Harry walked to and from work. Sometimes he would stop briefly outside the window of the storefront and, with unfeigned curiosity, glance at the work that was taking place therein. The man that owned this shop seemed to be the antithesis of Mackay. A godless, vile man was he, and Harry sensed that his shop was run quite differently. Harry noticed that the man never struck the leather soles with so much as one blow from the hammer, but rather nailed them onto the shoe while they were still soaking wet.

Eureka! A bypass had been discovered to the nasty case of "cobbler's elbow" Harry was developing from all the unending (and apparently needless) blows to the leather with the hammer. But don't take it from me, let's hear the story in the first person, as Ironside picks up account and relays the following life lesson concerning the value of our work to God and the importance of doing all for the cause of Christ.

One day I ventured inside, something I had been warned never to do. Timidly, I said, "I notice you put the soles on while still wet. Are they just as good as if they were pounded?" He gave me a wicked leer as he answered, "They come back all the quicker this way, my boy!" Feeling I had learned something, I related the instance to my boss and suggested that I was perhaps wasting time in drying out the leather so carefully. Mr. Mackay stopped his work and opened his Bible to the passage, "Whatsoever ye do, do all to the glory of God." "Harry," he said, "I do not cobble shoes just for the four bits and six bits (fifty or seventy-five cents) that I get from my customers. I am doing this for the glory of God. I expect to see every shoe I have ever repaired in a big pile at the judgment seat of Christ, and I do not want the Lord to say to me in that day, 'Dan, this was a poor job. You did not do your best here.' I want Him to be able to say, 'Well done, good and faithful servant.'" Then he went on to explain that just as some men are called to preach, so he was called to fix shoes, and that only as he did this well would his testimony count for God. [2]

Chiming in on the issue of secular versus sacred and giving our best to God, Bob Jones, Sr. astutely said, *Life is not divided into the secular and sacred. All ground is holy ground, and every bush is a burning bush.* Remember the whole burning bush conversation that took place between God and Moses? *And he said, Draw not nigh hither: put off thy shoes from off thy feet, for the place whereon thou standest is holy ground.* (Exodus 3:5) Holy ground? You have got to be kidding; Moses was on the underside of the backside of the long since forgotten side of the desert! Ground which is sacred? Somebody please tell me to smile, because some descendant of Alan Funt must surely be close at hand with the candid cameras rolling, capturing the whole sordid gag on film. And yet to a Holy, very much non-secular God, everything is to be held sacred. All pursuits matter very much to God and He cares how we carry them out. *And whatsoever ye do in word or deed, do all in the name of the Lord Jesus, giving thanks to God and the Father by him.* (Colossians 3:17) Take note that the greatest follower of Christ ever, the Apostle Paul, gave a decisive thumbs-down to a 2D perspective on living which wrongly divides the secular from the sacred.

LIFE IN 3D

If the thought begins to encroach that this whole epilogue lacks much in personal relevance, I assure you that this is not much ado about nothing. The reason why all this is so very significant in the context of finding, following, and finishing God's call for your life, is that when we take down the self-fabricated construction cones in our mind dividing the two, we release the stranglehold that the secular has held for far too long on the sacred. And in so doing, we permit the sacred the free reign God intended, allowing it to permeate each and every remarkable, as well as routine, aspect of our lives, forever shifting our perspective around why we do what we do.

Is there anything sacred about a born again child of God who underwrites insurance, operates a bulldozer, raises cattle, writes human resource policies, drives a cab, prepares tax returns, fills in potholes, drafts engineering specs, manages sales or does HVAC repair? Yes! Yes! And again, Yes! If that is God's calling for them and they wake up each day dead-set on doing such for the glory of God. All these fields and more are holy and they are sacred indeed. I like A.W. Tozer's weighing in, *We must do worldly jobs, but if we do them with sanctified minds, they become offerings to God.*

When we put on our 3D glasses and look at things in the biblical light and perspective in which God does, we'll no longer subdivide our lives in such a way that keeps God in the nosebleed seats for 98% of our weekly existence. As we continue to view each moment and every aspect of daily living as sacred, we'll see God make His way from the nosebleed seats in Section 317/Row YY of our lives, down to the Owner's box, where He rightfully belongs.

Right now, at this very moment, you are as close to God as you want to be. *Draw nigh to God, and he will draw nigh to you.* (James 4:8) When we take a little step of faith towards God, He moves a giant leap towards us, because His stride is a lot bigger than

---〰〰---

Right now, at this very moment, you are as close to God as you want to be.

---

ours. And our adopting the viewpoint that everything in this life is sacred to God, and to us, is no small step of faith. Friend, you have a field. And in God's eyes, that field has long since been considered very much sacred. Isn't it about time it was so in your eyes?

Patience has its limits. Take it too far, and it's cowardice.
~George Jackson

Destiny is no matter of chance. It is a matter of choice. It is not a thing to be waited for; it is a thing to be achieved.
~William Jennings Bryan

When written in Chinese, the word 'crisis' is composed of two characters. One represents danger and the other represents opportunity.
~John Fitzgerald Kennedy

The greatest pleasure in life is doing what people say you cannot do.
~Walter Bagehot

Far better is it to dare mighty things, to win glorious triumphs, even though checkered by failure . . . than to rank with those poor spirits who neither enjoy much nor suffer much, because they live in a gray twilight that knows not victory nor defeat.
~Theodore Roosevelt

CHAPTER #3

Consider the Field

She considereth a field, and buyeth it: with the fruit of her hands she planteth a vineyard. (Proverbs 31:16)

Y ou've been there. A thousand and one times you have most definitely been there. There you are in the checkout line at the supermarket, and as you patiently wait your turn to unload the contents of your cart on the conveyor belt, your eyes begin to peruse your confined surroundings. The first thing that catches your eyes are the tabloids, as the shock and awe headlines leap off the page in a successful attempt to garner your attention. Lose 25 pounds by the weekend. Another celebrity marriage. Another celebrity break-up. UFO's surround the skies of downtown Los Angeles with alien abductions reported (actually, this one just might have some credence). Yet another Elvis sighting-this time like a blurred, amateurish photo of the backside of Sasquatch in the woods, the King is caught on camera wolfing down a scone as he slurps on what appears to be a skinny, double shot, venti iced Carmel Macchiato as he struts out of a downtown Memphis Starbucks sporting some pretty sweet blue shoes (presumably suede).

Feeling pretty current on world events, your eyes shift and manage to catch the rows and rows of strategically placed snacks. A candy bar is nowhere to be found on your shopping list; neither are the breath mints or fingernail clippers and yet, on impulse, into the basket they go. Those within the field of retail merchandising have appropriately dubbed this transaction an "impulse buy;" that is to say, the purchase of these items was not pre-meditated. Rather, it took place instantaneously with little or no consideration. And such impulse buys for a stick of beef jerky, a bottle of pain reliever, or some spearmint chewing gum are part and parcel of everyday living. These are not decisions which require much deliberation. Whether you grab a ChapStick tube or a tub of Carmex lip balm is not a decision that is apt to haunt you with regret the rest of your days (or even the rest of that day). No sleep will be lost tonight because you did not consider through fasting and prayer whether to toss a package of Energizer or Duracell brand AA batteries into the cart. But it seems within the Christian faith, that there is not nearly enough careful, deliberate, soul searching reflection when it comes to matters of much greater consequence-matters such as finding a field or vocational calling for your life.

STEP BY STEP

As we read the account of the godly example of a lady who is referred to as the "Proverbs Thirty-One Woman," one soon discovers the caliber of person she is and the character traits she possesses. Endearing attributes such as faithfulness to her husband, shameless of her role as a mom and believes it to be of the utmost importance and one of her highest callings, generosity towards others and tireless in her efforts to be a blessing to her family. All of this and more, as kindness and wisdom flow in the wake of her every move. All of these marks of integrity, and much more which scripture says of her, declares that she is a woman who lives life intentionally and with due consideration. Everything about her affirms that she is a purposeful, deliberate lady who is very much not contented to go about her day, much less her life, simply "winging it". We see in verse sixteen that before she buys the field, she very carefully considers it. Unlike many of her contemporaries, she is not one given to impulse buying. While this may be the first parcel of land she has bought, it most definitely is not the first field she has carefully considered. This buying decision was some time in the making and an utterly fatigued real estate agent must have been at her wits' end, having all but run out of every last available listing in the MLS to show her.

Time and again in scripture, God's Spirit impresses upon individuals to consider, meditate, look upon, and invest of themselves in their fields.

———————— ∿ ————————
God's Spirit impresses upon individuals to consider, meditate, look upon, and invest of themselves in their fields.
————————————————————

Let thine eyes be on the field. (Ruth 2:9)

Lift up your eyes, and look on the fields. (John 4:35)

Come, and let us go out into the field. (1 Samuel 20:11)

Come, my beloved, let us go forth into the field.
(Song of Solomon 7:11)

It's true that the context in each of the above scriptural references is that of a physical field-a parcel of land that God is attempting to heighten one's awareness towards. But often God seeks to kindle our mindfulness that He has a vocational field for us, a work of His hands to immerse ourselves in for His enduring glory. The call from on high begins with our careful consideration of His field for us. That is the first step of an amazing journey that God has in store. And while it is true that it is only the first of many to be taken, it is still a big deal. That first step is a milestone event. Parents and other family members get excited when their toddler takes his or her first steps. They capture videos from the event and hurriedly post it on social media sites and are quick to contact friends and other family members to let them know the big news. And everyone's heart is thrilled at the growth and transformation taking place.

In that same line of reasoning, is it really such a stretch to envision that when God's children cross a milestone life event, that our Heavenly Father also gets excited at His children taking their first steps and making forward progress in the faith? Unlike parents, our Heavenly Father in His foreknowledge knew exactly when this day would come. Nonetheless, it still brings joy to the very heart of God to see His children stepping out in faith and taking strides in obedience to His truth. *I have no greater joy than to hear that my children walk in truth.* (3 John 1:4)

Too many of us never actually cross that milestone in our thinking. Somewhere following high school, or perhaps after college, we settle into a job, get married, have a child (or two) get a mortgage (or two!) and find ourselves on a career path that we simply do not spot any marked exits from. And even if we did see a sign indicating an exit ahead, it can often feel as though life has us stuck bumper to bumper across six lanes of rush hour traffic on the 405 (or the 290, 465, 676, 395, 285 or whatever such numerical names those highly congested stretches of asphalt go by in your neck of the woods).

Or even worse than being sandwiched in traffic, is that we find ourselves going the wrong way on a one way street, against the flow of traffic. Like the account of the young man who was walking along a country road, and as he did, a farmer driving a wagon passed by. Without asking permission, the young man jumped upon the wagon and said, "I'm going to ride with you to Louisville." The farmer just looked at him and said nothing. They rode on for 10 miles. The young man began to feel uneasy. He turned to the farmer and said, "I say old pop, how much farther is it to Louisville?" The farmer replied, "If you keep in the direction you are going, it is about 25,000 miles; but if you get off and walk back the other way, it is only about sixteen miles—six miles from where you jumped on." [1]

I know that life is a highway, but sometimes we just jump on for a ride without first finding out where it is going to take us. God has the ride of our life mapped out for us already, and the onus is on us to make sure we hitch a ride to His wagon.

CAR WASHES AND ARCHERY RANGES: FINDING DIRECTION IN THE MOST UNLIKELY OF PLACES

For six wonderful years, I called a suburb in the upper northwest side of Houston home in the rapidly growing town of Cypress, Texas. An automated car wash had been newly built less than a mile from the house and I would frequent the wash quite often, as I never had to leave the comfort of my driver's seat.

After dropping in the token and pulling forward, there was that heavy-pressure spray coming from below to clean the underneath side of my vehicle. As the spray does its' dirty work, I have to continue pulling forward about twenty feet until the next step of the car wash initiates. Because of the heavy spray, it could be very hard to see where you are going. This is especially true in the winter time as the warm mist from below combines with the cool, crisp air above to form a dense fog of sorts. For this reason, the owner has installed an electronic sign displaying three arrows at the back of the bay. If I drift too far to the right, a left arrow flashes, indicating for me to turn in that direction. Ditto if I am drifting too far to the right. If I am dead on course, then there is an arrow signaling straight ahead, indicating to keep going forward in the direction I am going.

Even with the blinking arrows doing their thing and my car wipers humming in perfect unison as fast they possibly can, the under-spray can be so heavy that it is difficult to know which direction to steer. It is essential to maintain a steady, fixed focus on the directional arrows, for without such, the short distance I have to go could find me getting off track, running into the tire guard rails and moving forward with caution and uncertainty. Fortunately, in all the times that I have washed my car there, the arrows have proven to be a trusted, reliable source to guide me and have never *steered* me wrong (groan).

Like many aspects of life, the physical exercise in staying on track at the car wash has a spiritual equivalent of sorts. The many pressures and uncertainties of this life can often find us disoriented and not really knowing what step to take next, where to turn or which direction to go. It's not by coincidence that verses such as this one have been divinely placed in the Bible for our benefit, *Let thine eyes look right on, and let thine eyelids look straight before thee. Ponder the path of thy feet, and let all thy ways be established. Turn not to the right hand nor to the left.* (Proverbs 4:25-27)

God has a wonderfully designated path for us, and desires to lovingly guide us all along the unfamiliar way.

> *And I will bring the blind by a way that they knew not; I will lead them in paths that they have not known: I will make darkness light before them, and crooked things straight. These things will I do unto them, and not forsake them.* (Isaiah 42:16)

The Lord would have His children stay close by His side, so that we can hear the Holy Spirit whisper to us, *And thine ears shall hear a word behind thee, saying, This is the way, walk ye in it.* (Isaiah 30:21)

In an attempt to thwart this from happening, the enemy of our souls is constantly shooting under spray all around us in an effort to disorient and get us off track. The devil's under-spray can assume many different manifestations: selfishness, temptations, distractions, diversions, vanity, discouragement, and fear to name but a few. Numerous unwitting Christians proceed with recklessness through such challenges of life, not earnestly considering God's "directional arrows" or being sensitive to His "guardrails" placed for our protection and to guide us in the way that we should go.

Scripture also sounds a resolute warning to people who seek Him at only a superficial level. These are the folks who want just enough of Jesus to help them be successful or to overcome some obstacle, sickness, or other difficulties they are confronting at the present moment; but not so much of Him as to really interfere with the course of their lives. We make a tragic blunder when we seek God's direction half-heartedly or in an agenda-driven, self-serving manner. *But if from thence thou shalt seek the LORD thy God, thou shalt find him, if thou seek him with all thy heart and with all thy soul.* (Deuteronomy 4:29) The good news is that within your heart-of-hearts, if you have a resolve to do what God would have you to do, then you are apt to soon come across the FSBO (For-Sale-By-Owner) sign in God's chosen field for you.

Let's look at yet another account of scripture and see if there are any precepts that we can draw from when looking for His arrows. Young David was trying to determine the next right step in his life. He had been employed by his best friend Jonathan's father, King Saul, but it was something of an on again-off again kind of relationship. Donald Trump is a kingpin within the financial world today, and when he has had enough of someone who is on his payroll, he has been known to brashly shout out, "You're Fired!" Well, when King Saul grew weary of issuing David a W-2 form, on more than one occasion, he launched a javelin at him! After playing a couple rounds of dodge-javelin, David did not know what to do or which direction to turn. Does God want him to continue to stick-it out on in his present job, knowing he might literally get "stuck" if he does; or is God trying to move him on? We pick up the account in the twentieth chapter of 1 Samuel, as Jonathan speaks these words to his best friend, David.

*And I will shoot three arrows on the side thereof, as though I shot
at a mark. And, behold, I will send a lad, saying, Go, find out
the arrows. If I expressly say unto the lad, Behold, the arrows are
on this side of thee, take them; then come thou: for there is peace
to thee, and no hurt; as the LORD liveth. But if I say thus unto
the young man, Behold, the arrows are beyond thee; go thy way:
for the LORD hath sent thee away . . . And it came to pass in
the morning, that Jonathan went out into the field at the time
appointed with David, and a little lad with him. And he said
unto his lad, Run, find out now the arrows which I shoot. And as
the lad ran, he shot an arrow beyond him. And when the lad was
come to the place of the arrow which Jonathan had shot, Jonathan
cried after the lad, and said, Is not the arrow beyond thee? And
Jonathan cried after the lad, Make speed, haste, stay not. And
Jonathan's lad gathered up the arrows, and came to his master.
But the lad knew not any thing: only Jonathan and David knew
the matter.* (1 Samuel 20:20-22, 35-39)

While Jonathan was the one that pulled back the bowstring, verse
twenty-two tells us that it was the Lord that superintended the distance
of the arrows. Perhaps God has been shooting directional arrows in your
life in an effort to point you in the way which He would have you to
go. If so, you must be discerning and look past the under-spray the
enemy is shooting all around you. The challenge from scripture is to
carefully consider the field. *Wherefore be ye not unwise, but understanding
what the will of the Lord is.*
(Ephesians 5:17) Stop with the
brushing aside of the Holy
Spirit's guiding presence.
Remove any self-imposed
blinders to His leading. Be done with the finger pointing or resorting
to blame—shifting. Enough with having our eyes wide shut to the
direction in which God is so plainly leading.

---
*Wherefore be ye not unwise, but under-
standing what the will of the Lord is.*
(Ephesians 5:17)

THE STRENGTH OF A THREEFOLD CORD

We see the principle of strength in numbers clearly set forth in scripture. *And if one prevail against him, two shall withstand him; and a threefold cord is not quickly broken.* (Ecclesiastes 4:12) I don't think it is fair or biblically honest to always attempt to formulize scripture, and reduce the victorious Christian life to a paint-by-numbers approach. But since there is great stability afforded by three-legged stools and solid anchoring evidenced in threefold stakes, let's circle back around on the touch-and-go-landing we took in the previous chapter at Jeremiah 29 and take a closer look. In it, we will see that this passage contains bedrock truth for the Christian who desires more than anything to find God's calling.

<u>Cord #1: Serving God with all of our hearts through work.</u> *For I know the thoughts that I think toward you, saith the LORD, thoughts of peace, and not of evil, to give you an expected end.* (Verse 11)

I'll be honest and upfront. The following two cords are totally predictable. You're clever and I am confident that you will spot them coming from a mile away. No, "Aha" moment awaits you. But work? I'm guessing this cord came out of nowhere in your thinking and took you totally by surprise. God's "expected end" for each of us is further revealed and comes into more vivid detail when we serve Him right where we are. *Commit thy works unto the LORD, and thy thoughts shall be established.* (Proverbs 16:3) God gives clarity of mind to those who have a mind to work. (See Nehemiah 4:6)

In any successful weight loss program, there is found diet (not ingesting the wrong foods) and balanced nutrition (ingesting the right foods). Any trainer would tell you that while those are both needful and will take you a long way towards your goal, adding exercise will get you where you want to be faster. And so it is with working and serving God with all of our heart right where we are. Giving our best while working where God has us is like adding a daily spinning class to your weight loss efforts. Sure, it will cause you to break a sweat and wear you out-but it's a good kind of tired and in the long run, you'll sure be glad you did.

We will have more to say about work in chapter five, but suffice it to say that God is looking for laborers, *Then saith he unto his disciples, The harvest truly is plenteous, but the labourers are few; Pray ye therefore the Lord of the harvest, that he will send forth labourers into his harvest.* (Matthew 9:37-38) When we roll up our sleeves and serve God with all of our heart where we are at NOW, coupled with the next two cords mentioned below, He will show us the NEXT step.

<u>Cord #2: SEEKING God with all of our hearts in prayer.</u> *Then shall ye call upon me, and ye shall go and pray unto me, and I will hearken unto you.* (Verse 12)

Consider this a string around the finger, a reminder that the avenue to God and His will for our lives is paved through prayer. No casual kind of praying will do when it comes to getting a hold of God. We must be "all-in" and whole-hearted.

<u>Cord #3: SPENDING time with God with all of our Heart in His Word.</u> *And ye shall seek me, and find me, when ye shall search for me with all your heart.* (Verse 13)

While prayer is largely me talking to God, reading His Word is first and foremost God talking to me. *Thy word is a lamp unto my feet, and a light unto my path.* (Psalms 119:105) *The entrance of thy words giveth light; it giveth understanding unto the simple.* (Psalms 119:130) But just like prayer, no casual kind of Bible reading will do. Ever read an entire chapter or two (or ten) close your Bible and literally not have a clue as to what you just read? That's because our hearts were not in it and we were distracted.

UNDER NEW OWNERSHIP

There is a story from long ago where an old Scottish woman went from home to home across the countryside selling thread, buttons, and shoestrings. When she came to an unmarked crossroad, she would toss a stick into the air and go in the direction the stick pointed when it landed. One day, however, she was seen tossing the stick up several times. "Why do you toss the stick more than once?" someone asked. "Because," replied the woman, "it keeps pointing to the left, and I want to take the road on the right." She then dutifully kept throwing the stick into the air until it pointed the way she wanted to go.

The time for our self-will exerting itself in our lives has come and gone. *The night is far spent, the day is at hand: let us therefore cast off the works of darkness, and let us put on the armour of light.* (Romans 13:12) It is time to go. Go where He wants you to go. It is time to be. Be what He wants you to be. It is time to do. Do what He wants you to do. The Lord Jesus Christ did not endure the cruel death of the cross so that you and I could live any old way of our own choosing. No, He gave His life so that we might live afresh and new for Him. *Therefore if any man be in Christ, he is a new creature: old things are passed away; behold, all things are become new.* (2 Corinthians 5:17 He suffered and bled and died so that we might be have newness of life and live in light of it.

> It is time to go. Go where He wants you to go. It is time to be. Be what He wants you to be. It is time to do. Do what He wants you to do.

I have been privileged to call several different states home, including Indiana, Texas, Michigan, Ohio and Missouri. Every time we have moved, my wife and I believed we were following the Lord's leading the best we knew how, and yet every move was difficult. The relocation was difficult in the sense of having to say goodbye to dear friends and church families that we had come to know and love. The farewell bidding to familiar surroundings and amenities, chiefly our home and the many great family memories that were made in that place and the labor of love, prayer, and sweat that held it all together.

One such home of several we waved goodbye too stands out. With 3,200 blessed square feet, it had become our dream home and was a little bit of heaven on earth. The interior beauty and creature comforts of our home were rivaled only by the exceptional curb appeal of the stately exterior. A beautifully designed mosaic of brick and stonework enveloped the large two story structure, whose beauty was enhanced with pine trees that stretched high up into the south Texas sky and a professionally landscaped lawn with not so much as a trace of a solitary rogue weed.

And then amidst the most beautiful of residential settings, some real estate agent goes and drives deep into the soil of our lawn (and even deeper into our hearts) a repulsive looking "For Sale" sign. Dream over.

After nearly twenty years in the corporate world, the Lord had called me into full time ministry to preach the gospel. With that call, some of the creature comforts we had enjoyed would now be out of reach as a Pastor supporting a family of six. I never will forget closing day and the signing over of ownership papers. At the title company's office, my wife and I sat across the table from the buyer as we had done many times before, but this-well, this was different. What was at stake here was no ordinary signing. A line had been drawn in the sand concerning the direction of our lives and knowing this, we were willingly crossing over. A thick air of finality lingered heavy in the room that day, as my wife and I signed everything over to the new owner.

In the weeks to come, I would hear from former neighbors concerning changes that the new owner was making. He did what? He cut down that gorgeous tall pine tree in the front yard? You don't mean it! He ripped out all the new carpet on the first floor and put in wood flooring? Are you serious? He tore up most of the lush, weed-free Bermuda grass in the back yard and put in a huge swimming pool? Say it isn't so! (Ok, I actually have to give the thumbs-up to that improvement) But all the other remodeling changes, not so much. Who does he think he is, anyway? Oh. Oh, yeah. Almost forgot. He's the new owner.

In the wake of this life-altering decision and subsequent chain of events, I was reminded of some simple truths. While I owned the home, it was mine to do with as I pleased because as owner, I was the boss. But then I decided to sell it. On closing day when the new owner took possession, I turned over the deed, the schematics to the underground sprinkler system, and the key to the front door to him. The home is now his. He can make any changes he desires. He can do with it as he pleases. Perhaps I approve of what he is doing and his plans for the future, or maybe not; either way I have no viable say in the matter because the home is no longer mine. It's now his.

That's the way it must be with your life and mine. The truth behind 2 Corinthians 5:17 is that when we give our life to Christ, in effect, we turn over the title deed, the schematics to all our days ahead, and the keys of our life to Jesus-the new Owner. Anyone that ever genuinely came to Christ in the pages of scripture experienced such a life change. There were old things that were out and new things that were brought in. It is simply part and parcel of giving up ownership to that of another.

Instead of trying to hang onto the key and the ensuing saga and ongoing power struggle with our new Landlord, our time could be far better spent crying out to God as did Paul, *And I said, What shall I do, Lord? And the Lord said unto me, Arise, and go into Damascus; and there it shall be told thee of all things which are appointed for thee to do.* (Acts 22:10) The problem is, few Christians are willing to go to Damascus (where God wants us to go) because we are dead-set on making our way down towards Tarshish (where we want to go). Let me explain.

LIFE IN TARSHISH

Most everyone knows the account of Jonah and the whale. It stems from an old testament book bearing the same name, and consists of only four chapters. Even so, the story is unforgettable and the lessons from this prodigal prophet innumerable for he was the original, "I'll go where I want to go and do what I want to do" genre of rebel. God's directional arrows were unmistakably clear as He instructed Jonah to go to the city of Ninevah, and Jonah, well, Jonah went as far as anyone could go in the opposite direction.

> *Now the word of the LORD came unto Jonah the son of Amittai, saying, Arise, go to Nineveh, that great city, and cry against it; for their wickedness is come up before me. But Jonah rose up to flee unto Tarshish from the presence of the LORD, and went down to Joppa; and he found a ship going to Tarshish: so he paid the fare thereof, and went down into it, to go with them unto Tarshish from the presence of the LORD.* (Jonah 1:1-3)

Bible commentators agree to disagree on the exact interpretation and location of Tarshish. But some lean to the understanding that Tarshish was the area of land which today we know as the British Isles. If such is the case, Tarshish was not only the opposite direction of Ninevah; it was as far as one could go from that city in the then known world. Look at the progression, or more aptly the digression, of Jonah's decision making, evidenced in the third verse of chapter one.

He arose and fled—In completely the opposite direction that God was shooting His arrows.

He went down—"Down" is the direction our running from God will always take us.

He found a ship—Jonah looked for a way out and found it. Satan is ever so quick to come alongside and "help" us find a way out of God's will for our lives.

He paid fare—There was a cost involved in his disobedience, and he showed no signs of suffering from buyer's remorse.

He went—He sealed his fate. He could have easily turned back at any time and God would have not chastised him. Jonah was a living testimony to the fact that sin will take you farther than you ever intended to go, keep you longer than you ever wanted to stay, and cost you more than you ever imagined to pay.

But then, the grace of God confronted Jonah in a great storm (Jonah 1:4-16) and ultimately in the most unlikely of physical manifestations-a great fish. (Jonah 1:17) Recognizing these events as the undeniable hand of God, Jonah never did quite make it to Tarshish. Reading through the second chapter, it is clear that Jonah came to a fork in the road in his own life, and at long last he put down the stick that he previously had kept tossing up in the air when he came to such junctions and just did what God wanted him to do. He finally came to the realization that running from God is always a losing race. We can spend our entire life running, and yet wherever our worn out, about-to-fall-apart running shoes should take us, God is still there.

> Running from God is always a losing race.

> *Whither shall I go from thy spirit? or whither shall I flee from thy presence? If I ascend up into heaven, thou art there: if I make my bed in hell, behold, thou art there. If I take the wings of the morning, and dwell in the uttermost parts of the sea; Even there shall thy hand lead me, and thy right hand shall hold me.*
> (Psalm 139:7-10)

Which direction is your life headed right now? Tarshish, representing life done your way; or Ninevah, symbolizing life lived God's way? Someone has once wisely put it, *Even more important than where you stand, is which direction it is that you are going.* Many saved, born again, on-their-way-to-Heaven Christians are racking up a ton of frequent flyer miles with their many trips en route to Tarshish.

> ❧
> *Even more important than where you stand, is which direction it is that you are going.*

I appreciate true, time-tested expressions like, *Where God guides, He provides, God's will done, God's Way will never lack God's supply,* and *God Pays For What He Orders.* But God never sent Jonah to Tarshish, and neither is He giving you the nod to catch the next flight out and head that wayward direction either. Like Jonah then, the fare to Tarshish today is steep, and we are on our own when picking up the tab for that one. Still, the greatest cost for us while living in the land of Tarshish is not so much the financial as it is the time wasted, the opportunities lost, and relational distancing from God while we are living the life of a fugitive on the run.

For the Christian travelling through life the wrong way on a one-way street, one of your most gripping fears should be to celebrate your sixtieth, seventieth, or even eightieth birthday and to find that you are still running in the opposite direction of the dream God gave you. Diane Ackerman was once quoted as having said, *I don't want to get to the end of my life and find that I have just lived the length of it. I want to have lived the width of it as well.* There are those individuals whose lives seem to have been cut tragically short, but most folks live life the full *length* of it. How exceptionally rare and precious it is to witness a Christian man or woman experience the full *width* of God's plan for their lives as well.

HUMAN HISTORY IN A NUTSHELL

The entire history of world events, since the time of Creation up to the present, could be boiled down to this one simple, profound, statement: The Spirit of God moving in fulfillment of God's plan and Satan moving in opposition to that plan. What a succinct yet insightful summation, and if such is true for all of God's creation, how much more the case concerning the plan for His chief creation, mankind.

The first half of this bold claim declares that God has a perfect plan in mind for you that has been in play since eternity past, *For we are his workmanship, created in Christ Jesus unto good works, which God hath before ordained that we should walk in them.* (Ephesians 2:10)

The second half of the same statement adds the sobering reality that Satan is relentless with his intent to thwart God's perfect plan for your life and to have you comfortably settle into the densely populated metroplex of mediocrity. *Be sober, be vigilant; because your adversary the devil, as a roaring lion, walketh about, seeking whom he may devour.* (1 Peter 5:8) Satan's ongoing work of sidetracking and sabotage is displayed in the gospel of Mark, *The sower soweth the word. And these are they by the way side, where the word is sown; but when they have heard, Satan cometh immediately, and taketh away the word that was sown in their hearts.* (Mark 4:14-15) Don't be mistaken. Satan isn't content only to snatch away the seed of the Gospel that has

> Satan is relentless with his intent to thwart God's perfect plan for your life and to have you comfortably settle into the densely populated metroplex of mediocrity.

been sown in a sinner's hearts; he also wages war in the hearts of Christians in an attempt to hush the voice that God speaks to His children through the indwelling presence of the Holy Spirit. And on either battle front, Satan not only strives to silence God's voice to us, he schemes to replace that commanding voice with his own corrupt voice, the voice of the world.

TRAVELLING THROUGH VANITY FAIR

In John Bunyan's classic allegorical literary work, *The Pilgrim's Progress*, the same sort of pleasurable trappings we learned of from Odysseus and the land of the Lotus-Eaters, hold their victims captive in the town of Vanity. In that futile town a daily festival is held that is known as Vanity-fair. The main character, Christian, travels through this place of amusement entirely given over to vanity, and takes it all in. Bunyan describes the scene for us.

> *. . . a fair wherein should be sold of all sorts of vanity, and that it should last all the year long. Therefore at this fair are all such merchandise sold as houses, lands, trades, places, honours, preferments, titles, countries, kingdoms; lusts, pleasures, and delights of all sorts, such as, whores, bawds, wives, husbands, children, masters, servants, lives, blood, bodies, souls, silver, gold, pearls, precious stones, and what not. And moreover at this fair, there is at all times to be seen juggling, cheats, games, plays, fools, apes, knaves, and rogues, and that of every kind . . . This fair, therefore, is an ancient thing, of long standing, and a very great fair"*[2]

Whether travelling through the allegorical city known as Vanity Fair, or canvassing the mythical land of the Lotus Eaters, or making our way through the everyday encounters and trappings of life in this 21st century; the warning signs are clearly posted for all who care to read and heed.

> *Love not the world, neither the things that are in the world. If any man love the world, the love of the Father is not in him. For all that is in the world, the lust of the flesh, and the lust of the eyes, and the pride of life, is not of the Father, but is of the world.*
> (1 John 2:15-16)

HOW'S YOUR AIM?

The year was 2004. The city was Athens, Greece. The setting was the 28th Olympiad, and American Olympic Rifle Shooter, Matt Emmons, had the gold medal in his sights . . . literally. He was one shot away from claiming victory in the 50-meter three-position rifle event. He didn't even need a bull's-eye to win. To take home the gold, his final shot merely needed to strike somewhere on the target. For an Olympian level athlete, this was a 'gimme.' It was just about the equivalent of a golf ball resting on the edge of the cup at a stop on the PGA Tour and Ernie Ells waltzing up and tapping it in to win the round. If such a gesture of sportsmanship was within his power to wield, I am sure that silver medal contender, Jia Zhanbo of China, would have told Matt, "Pick it up." This was a sure thing, if ever there was one in Olympic competition. The coveted gold medal was well within reach, as the Olympic band blew saliva out of their brass instruments while warming up to play, "The Star Spangled Banner" in recognition of pending USA gold. No doubt much of his life, at least for the past several years, had been spent in painstaking efforts to reach this point in this competition.

Matt's finger tightened firmly on the trigger. He took careful aim and fired. Under normal circumstances, the shot probably would have received a score of 8.1, much more than enough for a gold medal. But these circumstances were anything but normal. In what was described as "an extremely rare mistake in elite competition," with all the world watching on, Emmons took aim, fired, and his bullet hit the target with the blow intended. Unfortunately the intended blow struck the wrong target. Emmons stood in lane two and squarely hit the target that just so happened to reside in lane three. His aim-Dead on. His accuracy-Textbook. His target-Not so much.

Just in case one's interest is piqued at what kind of score is given to hitting the bull's eye of a wrong target in Olympic competition, here's your answer. Zero. Nada. Zilch. Null. Zip. So instead of standing on top of the podium and through tears, Emmons seeing the proud display of the beloved stars and stripes amidst chants of, "USA! USA! USA!"-it was the Chinese national anthem that rang out that fateful day. The flag unfurled was a sea of red, not the familiar stars and stripes which grace Old Glory. Maybe Emmons was a bit teary eyed, just not the way he had hoped. For you see, Emmons took the whole scene in from the bleachers, not the podium, as he ended up in medal-less eighth place.

Heartbreaking? Yep. Sobering? Understatement of the year. Worst sucker punch ever? It has my vote. But what was the rarest of Olympiad anomalies for one individual, is a common occurrence in the lives of countless followers of the Lord Jesus Christ. For every day, in newspapers across the country, obituaries are printed of men and women whose lives could be accurately summed up with the sobering headline: *Her aim was spotless, her shot was faultless, and her target was thoughtless.* Christians everywhere are aiming at the wrong life's target and hitting the bull's-eye. Dr. Charles Keene of Bearing Precious Seed Ministries succinctly put it like this, *I am not afraid of being a failure. I am afraid at being a success at something God is not interested in.*

> *I am not afraid of being a failure. I am afraid at being a success at something God is not interested in.*

There are numerous, "successful" Christians who, over the course of their lives, garner the attention and wonderment of those around them. But the issue is this; were they successful in things that God cares about? Did they light up the bull's-eye of the right target? Did they live out each and every day to its God-commissioned fullest, faithfully working in their field to achieve the calling of God upon their life? Take it from Matt Emmons-world class accuracy is of no earthly (or heavenly) value if the target in your sights is wrong. Consider your field.

PART II

Following God's Call

Opportunity comes like a snail, and once it has passed
you, it changes into a fleet rabbit and is gone.
~Arthur Brisbane

You are younger today than you ever will be again. Make use of it.
~Anonymous

If you can find a path with no obstacles, it
probably doesn't lead anywhere.
~Frank A. Clark

We are continually faced by great opportunities
brilliantly disguised as insoluble problems.
~Anonymous

The greatest mistake you can make in life is to be
continually fearing you will make one.
~Elbert Hubbard

CHAPTER #4

Buy the Field

*She considereth a field, and buyeth it: with the fruit of her hands
she planteth a vineyard.* (Proverbs 31:16)

FIELD OF DREAMS

In the 1989 movie "Field of Dreams," Iowa corn farmer, Ray Kinsella (played by Kevin Costner) plows under acres upon acres of his life-sustaining corn crop in order to build a baseball field because a "voice" speaks the following words to him, *If you build it, he will come.* The call to Ray was to build a baseball field, and the problem with "building it" was that the corn had already been planted. Understandably, Ray needed the income from harvesting the crop to keep his farm from going under. So, he is faced with the dilemma of either holding onto his field of dreams and the likelihood of losing it all; or leaving the corn alone and salvaging the remains of the only life he had ever known. Eventually, Ray does give in to the voice and plows under the corn, constructing a baseball field where lush, mortgage-paying, life-sustaining corn once stood tall. Alas, nothing happens. No one comes. Whoever "he" is, he's definitely late for dinner and despite all the dramatic build-up and promises, "he" is a big, fat no show.

It was near this point in the movie that Ray's brother-in-law, sounding an awful lot like one of Job's friends, counsels him with these words, *How could you plow under your major crop? You're going to lose your farm, pal.* Then, when things appeared beyond hope and all seemed lost, in grand fashion, enter Shoeless Joe Jackson from the Chicago Black Sox. In the face of overwhelming odds, Ray held onto the field of his dreams and witnessed his dream come true.

The point of all this is that once you have considered a field carefully, once you see that your treasure has been buried there, and once your heart has been firmly planted in the field as well-BUY IT. BUY THE FIELD! Stop with the waffling, contingency planning, second-guessing, and the endless "what-if" scenarios and buy the field. *How long will ye halt between two opinions?* (1 Kings 18:21) Stop kicking the tires already and step out in faith and do what God would have you to do.

WILL POWER

One such man that could never be found tarrying for long between two opinions was William Borden. In 1904, Borden graduated from a Chicago area high school, and as a graduation present, his parents gave him a trip around the world. Literally. As the young man traveled through Asia, the Middle East, and Europe, he felt a growing burden for those who had never heard the saving gospel of Jesus Christ. Obedient to the vision and all that he had taken in over the course of his travels young Will drafted a letter home about his desire to become a missionary. In response to that note, more than one friend expressed disbelief that Will had determined to throw his life away as a missionary. Reflecting on his decision and the reception of others towards it, Borden wrote two simple words in the back of his Bible: "No Reserves"

Will would go on to college at Yale, and during those years he continued to grow in the things of the Lord. One day he made a simple but profound entry in his personal journal: *Say 'no' to self and 'yes' to*

Jesus every time. Borden did exactly that. His witness for the Lord Jesus Christ on campus and his inspiration of others to make their lives count for God was incredibly forceful.

One of his classmates said of him: *He certainly was one of the*

Say 'no' to self and 'yes' to Jesus every time.

strongest characters I have ever known, and he put backbone into the rest of us at college. There was real iron in him, and I always felt he was of the stuff martyrs were made of, and heroic missionaries of more modern times. By the way, someone who follows the call of God for their life and has some iron in their backbone still attracts followers, and inspires others to greater things.

Borden's missionary call became refined and settled down to the Muslim Kansu people in China. Upon graduation from Yale, Borden was true to his call to missions and turned down some lucrative, high-paying job opportunities. In his Bible, next to his previous entry of *No reserves,* he wrote two more words: *No retreats.*

William Borden went on to do graduate work at Princeton Seminary in New Jersey, and when he had finished his studies at Princeton, he set sail for China. It was on his heart to work with unreached Muslims, and so he stopped first in Egypt to study Arabic. While there, literally half a world away from his family, friends, and the comforts of home, Will was diagnosed with spinal meningitis. Within a month, 25-year-old William Borden was dead. The testimony of his life story was not, however. When the news of Borden's death was cabled back to the U.S., the story was carried by nearly every major American newspaper. *A wave of sorrow went round the world. Borden not only gave [away] his wealth, but himself, in a way so joyous and natural that it [seemed] a privilege rather than a sacrifice,* wrote Mary Taylor in her introduction to his biography.

Prior to his death, Borden had written two more words in his Bible. Underneath *No reserves* and *No retreats*, he had penned one final thought. These two compelling words have served to inspire young men and women to yield their lives to the movement of missions. Two simple, dying last words: *No regrets.*

For the individual who accepts the challenge of scripture and willingly offers all of her earthly means back unto the Lord; that is certainly a rare and precious soul indeed.

> *Lay not up for yourselves treasures upon earth, where moth and rust doth corrupt, and where thieves break through and steal: But lay up for yourselves treasures in heaven, where neither moth nor rust doth corrupt, and where thieves do not break through nor steal: For where your treasure is, there will your heart be also.* (Matthew 6:19-21)

The follower of Jesus who not only is without any reserves, but also leaves no allowance for retreat or turning back on his decision, is truly a rare genre of Christian. *And Jesus said unto him, No man, having put his hand to the plough, and looking back, is fit for the kingdom of God.* (Luke 9:62) The Christian who gives away all his reserves, makes no provision for backtracking, and at the end of their life is free from any and all regrets for having done so and lived a life of complete surrender? Well now, that is amongst the rarest of all jewels within the entirety of Christendom.

Incidentally, after crippling financial losses in the early 1990's, and a leveraged buyout in 1995, Borden, Inc. divested itself of its various divisions and business entities. Considered the world's largest dairy and pasta producer at one time, Borden exited the corporate scene stage left and is no more. Over the span of more than a century and a half, no doubt many fine individuals sporting the last name of Borden were employed there, but odds are that we would be at a loss to recall the first name of even one of them. Will stood out and followed God's call on his life and bought the field. I believe young Borden was in good company with the likes of the Apostle Paul. From within his lonely Roman prison cell, Paul heard the executioner's steps drawing near as he penned these final, regret-free words.

For I am now ready to be offered, and the time of my departure is at hand. I have fought a good fight, I have finished my course, I have kept the faith: Henceforth there is laid up for me a crown of righteousness, which the Lord, the righteous judge, shall give me at that day: and not to me only, but unto all them also that love his appearing. (2 Timothy 4:6-8)

Would to God we would have a new generation of believers rise up and live their life with much the same galvanizing mantra: *No reserves. No retreats. No regrets.*

MEET AND GREET DEJA VU

Unlike Will Borden, many believers are completely sidetracked and go through life off target, never having lifted their eyes and prayerfully considered the sacred vocational field that God ordained for them long before they took their first breath. *Before I formed thee in the belly I knew thee; and before thou camest forth out of the womb I sanctified thee.* (Jeremiah 1:5) Praise God for those exceptional individuals, such as Will Borden and precious others, perhaps unknown to man but famous in the roll call of Heaven, whose lives are a wondrous inspiration to those around them (and to those who would one day follow them.) The lives and testimonies of such individuals serve as a catalyst for us today not only to consider the field but whatever the cost, by the grace of God, to pay the price and buy the field.

One such person of inspiration is the considerate woman from the thirty-first chapter of Proverbs that we were introduced to last chapter. Outside of a sermon each year on the second Sunday in May, we scarcely give her a second thought. Yet twenty-two verses in this one chapter of scripture are given to memorialize her for the godly woman she was and her many endearing attributes. One of the most revealing of her acclaim is found in verse sixteen, *She considereth a field, and buyeth it: with the fruit of her hands she planteth a vineyard.*

The challenge from the previous chapter was the giving ourselves to much prayerful consideration in search of what God would have us to do with this one life. But, the true rationale for why she has been brought to our attention yet again is not due to her careful consideration but the fact that she actually followed through, counted the cost, and bought the field. She wouldn't have received a footnote or so much as an honorable mention if scripture had spoken of her, *She considereth a field, but was one chiefly given to trifling delay and indecision, and alas, never did followeth through.* Careful, prayerful consideration serves to cultivate the soil of one's heart for a decision, a personal choice we each must make concerning the field that that has been revealed to us.

Volumes of lamentable commentaries could be written about Christians who came face to face with their God given destiny, tallied the costs, and got sticker shock; arriving at the conclusion that the asking price dangling from God's will for them was a little on the steep side, and they were not about to pay full MSRP (manufacturer suggested retail price). Not that they *couldn't* make the purchase mind you, but rather that they *wouldn't.*

God is calling us to higher living. When He leads us to the intersection of destiny and decision, as any good Father would, He simply asks His child to trust Him and take that next step of faith, and to buy the field. I really like the counsel that blogger and author of *Wrecked: When a Broken World Slams into Your Comfortable Life,* Jeff Goins has to say concerning the decision to act.

> When He leads us to the intersection of destiny and decision, He simply asks His child to trust Him and take that next step of faith.

There's nothing noble about an unlived life you thought of living. There's nothing romantic about audacious, unrealized dreams.

Nothing honorable about sacrifices made begrudgingly for a life you end up resenting. If you want to be something, why not begin by doing it? If you long to be a writer, then write. If an actor, then act. And if a runner, run. This is what determines all great endeavors—not just another interesting idea to talk about a coffee shop, but the decision to act, to move. One small step after another.

The time of kicking the tires, putting out one fleece after another and having your toes skim along the water's surface of what your life could be has come and gone. The clock is ticking with all the hosts of heaven looking on, as so very much hangs in the balance of your decision. When procrastination and neglect are tag-team wrestling with regret and missed opportunities, they become the four horsemen of the apocalypse of your life's calling. Count the costs. Pay the price. Buy the field. Do it now.

BLUE LIGHTS AND BLACK FRIDAYS

It was the summer of 1986. After my freshman year of college, I took a summer job at the K-Mart in Bay City, Texas, near the Gulf Coast. This was a small, insignificant store in a small, insignificant town from a bygone era. It was a no-frills Kmart, as they pretty much all were back then, not some BigK monstrosity where square footage measures well into the six digit range. There were no self-check-out stations with handy-dandy touch screens. There was a sum total of three, read 'em-and-weep, three check-out registers. While some products did have bar codes incorporated into their packaging back then, $3.25/hour minimum wage earning plebes such as myself had absolutely no clue what they were for, and we certainly had nothing save our good looks to scan them with at the check-out. Whatever the price was on the yellow sticker (green sticker if it was hardware, orange sticker if the item was from the sporting goods section, red sticker if it was clothing and blue sticker if it was health & beauty) is what we rang it up for.

For the handful of customers who paid by credit card, it was an enormous time sink, an almost unfathomable ordeal (or for any Mega-Mind fans, an ordeal without fathom.) First, the checker had to pull out a paper printout of the credit card industry's version of Santa's naughty list and make sure that the name on their photo ID was nowhere to be found on Visa or MasterCard's *Most Wanted*. Then, we had to get out the credit card swipe machine and the carbon copy paper form, swipe the card and have the customer write on the bottom of the slip their driver's license number, Social Security number (yes, that's right, we would actually ask customers to write in their SS# and they would actually do it!) and phone number (not their mobile number, as cell phones had yet to make it to the marketplace, but their house number, probably complete with a rotary dialing phone and a party line.) Amidst the backdrop of today's engineering marvels, the whole clumsy scene appears more than a little bit backwoods, technologically speaking.

But, we did have one thing back in the day that no BigK, Hyper-Walmart or Super-Target of today could in good conscious boast-that's right, the one, the only, blue light special. If ever there was a retail equivalent of the ESPY's, or a merchandising tantamount to the sporting hall of fames that grace Cooperstown, South Bend, and Canton; there would be due tribute to one of the chief retail marketing ploys of all time. The allure of the Blue Light Special was all the more persuasive because it was backed by the three most famous words known to man during that day. No, not, *I Love You, Sieze the Day, Pass the Biscuits, Praise the Lord or even L.O.L.* No, throughout the decade that was the 80's, the three most universally recognized words known to man were, *Attention Kmart shoppers.* When patrons of Kmart heard that sound, it only meant one thing. Somewhere lurking within the hallowed halls of the store, a deal was to be found. The item over which the blue light loomed large was for the most part inconsequential. Perhaps it was half-off all discontinued inventory of pet rocks, two dashboard bobble head Chihuahuas for a buck, buy-one-get-one Chia Pet hippopotamus while supplies last, or even forty percent off of the latest installment of Richard Simmons' *Sweatin' to the Oldies* dynasty on VHS (limit 1). Regardless, when the blue siren was boldly flashing its iconic beacon for all the world to see, or at least all the store, and those three infamous words rippled throughout the corridors of K-Mart land, I am here to tell you, it was on.

Granted, that was the '80's and much has changed in the years since. Chia Pets will set you back a bit more these days and they come in a truckload more varieties such as Chia SpongeBob, Chia Obama, and Chia Scooby and Shaggy, too. If you glance at the store shelves that once were saturated in Richard Simmons' jazzercise videos, you're more apt to see DVD's of P90X, Zumba or workout titles from the likes of fitness guru Jillian Michaels. Blue light specials have largely come and gone and given way to Black Friday (which is pretty much a sleep-deprived, day-long version of the blue light

When it comes to finding and fulfilling God's will for your life, there are no flashing blue sirens, door busters, or early bird specials.

special across the entire retail marketplace). Ours is the culture ever in trivial pursuit of a deal. But when it comes to finding and fulfilling God's will for your life, there are no flashing blue sirens, door busters, or early bird specials. God's will and His best for your life can never be found at rock-bottom discounted prices, and no clearance tags will ever dangle from something so precious.

DEAL OR NO DEAL

To follow the will of God for our life is a monumental, life-long adventure. It's no small wonder that the cautionary message of scripture before embarking upon such a noble quest is given in Luke's gospel.

> *For which of you, intending to build a tower, sitteth not down first, and counteth the cost, whether he have sufficient to finish it? Lest haply, after he hath laid the foundation, and is not able to finish it, all that behold it begin to mock him, Saying, This man began to build, and was not able to finish.* (Luke 14:28-30)

This something-for-nothing mindset which riddles present-day thinking is foreign to the legends in scripture that made their lives count for the glory of God. In the aftermath of King David's senseless census, seventy-thousand valiant men of Israel fell to pestilence in a single day. To bring an end to the plague, King David was instructed to erect an altar which would serve as both a reminder to the consequences of man's sin and also the goodness of God in His deliverance.

As King, David held sway over vast holdings including much land, God could have instructed him to break ground on any spot of thousands of acres which either he/the nation of Israel already held in their possession. But through a little known prophet named Gad, the Lord instructed David to set up this altar at the spot where the angel of the Lord had appeared. That location just happened to be a threshing floor which belonged to a Jebusite man named Ornan. David and his envoy approached Ornan.

> *Then David said to Ornan, Grant me the place of this threshing floor, that I may build an altar therein unto the LORD: thou shalt grant it me for the full price: that the plague may be stayed from the people. And Ornan said unto David, Take it to thee, and let my lord the king do that which is good in his eyes: lo, I give thee*

*the oxen also for burnt offerings, and the threshing instruments
for wood, and the wheat for the meat offering; I give it all. And
king David said to Ornan, Nay; but I will verily buy it for the full
price: for I will not take that which is thine for the LORD, nor
offer burnt offerings without cost.* (1 Chronicles 21:22-24)

Did you catch it? With the most noble of intentions, and eerily
sounding a bit like comedian turned game show host Howie Mandel,
Ornan essentially says, *David, your money is no good here. What's mine
is yours. You want to buy my place and offer a sacrifice to God? Well I am
prepared to make you an offer that you simply can't refuse. As a gift, no
strings attached, I want to give you this threshing floor and all that you see.
In fact, to sweeten the pot a bit, I have a prize bullock out grazing on the
back forty that the Mrs. and I were going to butcher next week, but you can
have it for your sacrifice. But wait, that's not all; if you act fast, I'll even
throw in all these threshing instruments which will make great kindling
wood to light the fires upon which your sacrifice will be offered.*

To this well meant gesture of unmerited generosity, David looks
Howie, uh, I mean Ornan, squarely in the eyes and sternly states,
Thanks, but no thanks. David restrained himself from slapping the iconic
red "deal" button and proceeded to slam shut its protective acrylic box,
as he unreservedly exclaimed, *No deal!* David would not accept such
generosity. More to the point, he could not in good conscience offer up
something to God as a sacrifice which cost him absolutely nothing.

What a striking contrast to the, *you won't believe the deal I got*
modern day mindset. Utilizing such contemporary negotiating tactics,
David would have been better served by telling him that his price wasn't
even in the ballpark, rather than been the one to break the news that
Ornan's asking price was way below the market value on neighboring
comps. David should have acted coy, sending the message that there
were no less than half a dozen other prominent, more favorable sites
that are currently in his consideration mix. David would have been
wise for his countenance to signal a rather disinterested, unimpressed

posture in the property which Ornan held the title deed to. Instead, he was overtly transparent. His approach was, this is the property God told me to get; therefore this is the property I want and I will pay top dollar for it, nothing less. End of discussion. David was quite keen that this threshing floor was God's will, and as such, he knew that there is always a cost to be counted and a price to be paid.

What David could not have possibly known, however, was that there was infinitely more at stake here than meets the eye. The site of Ornan's threshing floor was strategic in God's plan for His people, in that it was situated high upon Mount Moriah. Long before this parcel of land was to be employed in the threshing of wheat; it was a place of sacrifice as it is believed to have been the exact site where Abraham offered his son Isaac to the Lord as a burnt sacrifice (A foreshadowing of the once-and-for-all sacrifice for sin that God the Father would make through His Son, Jesus Christ). Again and again in scripture, there is a connection between Moriah and this matter of sacrifice, for this was not the first, nor would it be the last, altar to be built on this very site. In the generation that would follow David, his son Solomon would hold a ribbon cutting ceremony to end all such ceremonies on this same sacred dirt for the newly constructed Solomon's Temple. *Then Solomon began to build the house of the LORD at Jerusalem in mount Moriah, where the LORD appeared unto David his father, in the place that David had prepared in the threshingfloor of Ornan the Jebusite.* (2 Chronicles 3:1) Are you beginning to see some of the moving parts here and connect the dots?

As if all of that those prior linkages were not eyebrow raising enough, prophetically speaking, this same square footage in present day Jerusalem will also be the site where demolition crews will one day roll in, reduce to rubble the Mosque of Omar (a.k.a., the Dome of the Rock). This will pave the way for the construction of the third temple to be built during the not so distant future period of time commonly referred in Bible prophecy circles as, the tribulation period.

With all of this in mind, we can now begin to see how a flashing blue light situated prominently above the entrance to Ornan's threshing floor would mitigate the sacred nature of what had taken place, what was taking place, and what will one day take place there. In the midst of it all, David couldn't possibly see the totality of what was on the line. Sure he was able to put the pieces together with how this one wrong, through disobedience, would forever impact seventy-thousand men and their grieving families. But he could not have fathomed how that one wrong made right through obedience, was instrumental to what God was orchestrating and would forever benefit and impact countless others. By the way, neither could Will Borden, or hundreds of other heroes of the faith whose names and stories of service and surrender to the Lord Jesus Christ could be inserted here.

Feel a bit like it is your vision that is impaired, and that you can't see the beginning from the end? Dumbfounded as to why God is prompting you to take to heart the plea of the great hymn *Trust and Obey?* Speechless that He desires for that chorus to be far more than worshipful words sung on Sunday and make them words that you live by each and every day of the week? Pick your head up-you're in good company. Perhaps those waiting on the other end of your obedience are just as numerous as those who were doing likewise as David came to the great crossroads in his life. Let's bring an end to the domineering stalemate that has placed shackles on your life, trust and obey God come what may and step out as an act of unwavering faith and buy the field.

Follow the grain in your own wood.
~Howard Thurman

A man is not old until regrets take the place of dreams.
~John Barrymore

Too many people are thinking of security instead of opportunity. They seem more afraid of life than death.
~James F. Byrnes

The great thing in this world is not so much where you stand, as in what direction you are moving.
~Oliver Wendell Holmes

CHAPTER #5

Work the Field

She considereth a field, and buyeth it: with the fruit of her hands
she planteth a vineyard. (Proverbs 31:16)

For Korean fisherman Kim Yong-Chul, that day in July of 2007 started off like most any other. He made his way from his house to the harbor in the small fishing village of Taean, some sixty miles southwest of the capitol city of Seoul. He climbed aboard his small fishing vessel, made ready the nets, hoisted up anchor and set sail into the Yellow Sea, hopeful of a great haul of Webfoot Octopus. The unwieldy sea creature is considered a delicacy in Korea and select countries throughout the eastern Pacific Rim.

His hopes were realized as he did in fact haul in such a marine animal, but he pulled up far more from the Yellow Sea that fateful day, for attached to the octopus' tentacles were chards of antique pottery. Between what he brought up that day and subsequent dive expositions, some thirty bowls would be recovered. His treasure dated back to the twelfth century, during the period when the Koryo Dynasty ruled over the Korean peninsula. One fisherman's ordinary day at the office proved to be quite extraordinary and is hailed as one of the great undersea discoveries of modern times.

JUST ANOTHER DAY IN THE LIFE OF

For Kim Yong-Chul, the day-in and day-out faithfulness of working his field had, in the most unsuspecting of moments, an immense payday. Our reward for steady commitment to working in the field God would have for us is not the stuff that makes headline news, nor is it likely to catapult us to great wealth and fame overnight. But the reality is that incredible life rewards, both of the tangible and intangible variety, await the diligent worker who each day faithfully rolls up her sleeves, is not afraid to get dirt under her fingernails, and labors in her Father's field.

For the migratory farm worker, who goes from place to place in search of seasonal work, his lot is often rather uninspiring because of the hard work, long hours, and relatively low pay. But the God who beckons us to, *Take my yoke upon you . . . For my yoke is easy, and my burden is light* (Matthew 11:29-30) is no such taskmaster. He is a God that will be indebted to no man and faithfully rewards those who labor for Him. What kind of rewards? Well, Paul writes about our laboring in the field for Christ in his first letter to the church at Corinth.

> *I have planted, Apollos watered; but God gave the increase. So then neither is he that planteth any thing, neither he that watereth; but God that giveth the increase. Now he that planteth and he that watereth are one: and every man shall receive his own reward according to his own labour. For we are labourers together with God: ye are God's husbandry, ye are God's building. According to the grace of God which is given unto me.*
> (1 Corinthians 3:6-10)

From this one account alone, let us consider six rewards for faithfulness in our field.

Reward #1: Expending Ourselves for God's glory
I have planted. (Vs 6a)

It has been stated that this world is full of willing people—some willing to work; others willing to let them work! It is both exhilarating and exhausting at the same time to serve the Lord with all of our heart, soul, and mind as the scriptures have commanded us to do. We all wake up each morning with the same opportunity to use the day in service to God, or we can choose a far less lofty aim. It seems the familiar statement really is true: *Only two choices on the shelf; serving God or serving self.* In theory we know that serving God pays dividends in the sweet bye-and-bye; but practically, serving ourselves woos us with an immediate payout in the nasty here and now. Besides, on the surface serving God appears to require a whole lot more heavy lifting than serving self. And yet isn't that how "once in a lifetime opportunities" usually walk onto the scene of our lives, ever so cleverly disguised as hard work? *But let every man prove his own work, and then shall he have rejoicing in himself alone, and not in another. For every man shall bear his own burden.* (Galatians 6:4-5) Just as no man can ride the coattails of another man's experience of salvation, so it is with one's service.

> We all wake up each morning with the same opportunity to use the day in service to God, or we can choose a far less lofty aim.

Reward #2: Seeing God Multiply our Efforts
But God gave the increase. (Vs 6b)

The farmer tills the land, balances soil nutrition, plants the field, watches the weather forecasts, applies herbicides and other types of crop protection chemicals, irrigates and more. He does everything within his power to best enable his field to yield a bumper crop. Ultimately though, there are many variables outside of his control, highly influential factors such as weather temperatures and rainfall. There are no guarantees, as the Psalmist reminds us, *And sow the fields, and plant vineyards, which may yield fruits of increase.* (Psalms 107:37) That said, in His timing and in accordance with His will, it delights God to bless and multiply our diligent efforts for His glory.

Reward #3: Knowing Our Place
So then neither is he that planteth any thing, neither he that watereth; but God that giveth the increase. (Vss 6-7)

Our job is to work the work He has called us to do. The final tally on such labors is up to Him. *Faithful is he that calleth you, who also will do it.* (1 Thessalonians 5:24) We would do well to heed the counsel, *Work as if it all depended on you; pray as if it all depended on God.* That is our role—our place, and if we are not guarded, we can begin to buy into the lie that Satan whispers and our flesh so quickly acquiesces to.

Work as if it all depended on you; pray as if it all depended on God.

You may well have heard it whispered as well, the lie that God is really, really lucky to have us working for Him and on His team. But we must turn a deaf ear towards Satan's lies and instead allow scripture to bend our ear with these thoughts, *For if a man think himself to be something, when he is nothing, he deceiveth himself.* (Galatians 6:3) Do not be deceived friend. Verses six and seven above in 1 Corinthians 3 remind us that on our own, we are not anything

Whether in the classroom, workplace, athletic court or field, or even self-imposed expectations from within, we live in a world where there is constant pressure to perform. What a wonderful blessing to know that in God's harvest field, our call is one of faithfulness and to work and serve Him in humility. *By humility and the fear of the LORD are riches, and honour, and life.* (Proverbs 22:4) Only then can we confidently leave the results of such love-driven labor in His hands.

Reward #4: Serving Alongside Others
Now he that planteth and he that watereth are one. (Vs 8a)

I haven't always been a pastor or an author. Jeremiah had a hunch that he was called to be a prophet while he was still in the womb, but the recognition of my call came a little later in life. For a decade following graduating from college, I had an amazing job with a world leading pharmaceutical company, which also had a division which manufactured turf protection products such as insecticides and fungicides. For the first half of those ten years, my job was in sales and I visited superintendents at golf courses in an effort to inform them of our products and help evaluate whether they have a place within the superintendent's turf management program (And yes, I always traveled from course to course with my golf clubs in the back of the company car).

Many private golf courses and high-end public courses alike have a particular turf grass species called bent grass on their greens, tees, and often fairways as well. Golf course superintendents are paid to maintain the turf conditions at their course to the highest standards, and as one small part of that effort they must tackle different turf grass diseases that threaten the overall health and vigor of the turf. During my time in this field, there was an emerging disease pathogen complex that attacked bent grass, referred to as summer bent grass decline. For the most part, there was no single product, including the fungicides manufactured by the company I was employed by, that was successful in suppressing the pathogen. Superintendents did what they could from a soil management perspective (closely managing fertility, altering watering practices, raising mowing heights, and adding soil amendments) to keep their turf healthy through those times of high plant stress. Basically that was all that could be done.

But through research sponsored by university and manufacturers, a combination of two active ingredients, Mancozeb and Fosetyl-Al, proved to be highly effective. These active products were made by two multi-billion dollar global corporations who competed fiercely against each other, and yet collectively they worked together and seized the opportunity. Alone, their products were both largely ineffective against summer bent grass decline, but together, there was synergy. Conventional wisdom holds that 1+1=2. But in a synergistic setting, 1+1=3, as the collective sum is greater than the individual parts. These two companies partnered and did a lot in the way of co-marketing the two products and they won. The customer won. Hey, the grass even won! Basically everyone but the disease pathogen (and competing companies) came out the better for it. Why? Because they locked arms and worked together.

That spirit of oneness and working together is how God intended for it to be in our Christian life, *Stand fast in one spirit, with one mind striving together for the faith of the gospel.* (Philippians 1:27) Within the church, God has given individuals unique gifts. *And he gave some, apostles; and some, prophets; and some, evangelists; and some, pastors and teachers; For the perfecting of the saints, for the work of the ministry, for the edifying of the body of Christ.* (Ephesians 4:11-12) When working in isolation, these gifts will not go very far in making a difference for the cause of Christ and in the lives of others. But, laboring together alongside fellow Christians in local churches, there is synergy and unconventional math, whose equation could be best expressed as 1+1 = 3.

Reward #5: Equity
And every man shall receive his own reward according to his own labour. (Vs 8b)

We live in an unfair world. Lawlessness abounds and sometimes those who are wicked and do evil seem to get overlooked by authorities, while people striving to do right can appear at times to be overlooked by God. The prophet Isaiah described this well when he penned: *And judgment is turned away backward, and justice standeth afar off: for truth is fallen in the street, and equity cannot enter.* (Isaiah 59:14)

But verse eight reminds us that there will come a day when all things inequitable will come to a screeching halt. *Every man shall receive his own reward according to his own labour.* We have the assurance from scripture, *I will render to the man according to his work* (Proverbs 24:29) and that day of reckoning and the establishment of equity is described in the parable of the talents.

> *After a long time the lord of those servants cometh, and reckoneth with them. And so he that had received five talents came and brought other five talents, saying, Lord, thou deliveredst unto me five talents: behold, I have gained beside them five talents more. His lord said unto him, Well done, thou good and faithful servant: thou hast been faithful over a few things, I will make thee ruler over many things: enter thou into the joy of thy lord. He also that had received two talents came and said, Lord, thou deliveredst unto me two talents: behold, I have gained two other talents beside them. His lord said unto him, Well done, good and faithful servant; thou hast been faithful over a few things, I will make thee ruler over many things: enter thou into the joy of thy lord. Then he which had received the one talent came and said, Lord, I knew thee that thou art an hard man, reaping where thou hast not sown, and gathering where thou hast not strawed: And I was afraid, and went and hid thy talent in the earth: lo, there thou hast that is thine. His lord answered and said unto him, Thou wicked and slothful servant, thou knewest that I reap where I sowed not, and gather where I have not strawed: Thou oughtest therefore to have put my money to the exchangers, and then at my coming I should have received mine own with usury. Take therefore the talent from him, and give it unto him which hath ten talents.* (Matthew 25:14-28)

In this account, Jesus compares the kingdom of Heaven with a man who went on a long distanced journey. Before he did, he called in three of his servants and gave one five talents, another two talents, and the third servant one talent. The man with the five talents, as well as the one with the two, both were good stewards and wise in their dealings, and they doubled their money. Unfortunately, the soul that was given one talent did nothing with it, choosing to bury it in the dirt. He then had to stand before his master and give account of his doings, as will every one of us.

Reward #6: Working With God.

For we are labourers together with God. (vs 9a)

A final reward is an overwhelming one to meditate upon. By being diligent in working our field, we have joined forces with the Creator God of the universe. What an amazing thought! The invitation to labor together is open to all, as Jesus said, *Then saith he unto his disciples, The harvest truly is plenteous, but the labourers are few; Pray ye therefore the Lord of the harvest, that he will send forth labourers into his harvest.* (Matthew 9:37-38) We need to be reminded from time to time that together, God and I can do anything. Now that is synergy that blows the lid off of 1+1 =3!

Regardless of the vocational field, God rewards His faithful servants handsomely. He places great value on work, for God Himself is a worker. Of His many characteristics, it is the role of Worker that scripture first provides for us.

> *And on the seventh day God ended his work which he had made; and he rested on the seventh day from all his work which he had made. And God blessed the seventh day, and sanctified it: because that in it he had rested from all his work which God created and made.* (Genesis 2:3)

Some are under the faulty assumption that work is a curse and a result of the fall of Adam. But before the fall in the Garden of Eden, Adam had a job and was commissioned from God to work. *And the LORD God took the man, and put him into the garden of Eden to dress it and to keep it.* (Genesis 2:15) Jesus Himself weighed in on the high calling of work with these words, *I must work the works of him that sent me, while it is day: the night cometh, when no man can work.* (John 9:4) Regardless of the field, to be Christ-like, is to be a worker. What a joy and great reward it brings when we partner with Christ in His work and are co-laborers with Him.

CONSERVATION RESERVE PROGRAM

The Conservation Reserve Program, or CRP as it is better known in much of rural America, is a long-standing program with the noble aim of reducing topsoil erosion. In so doing, it conserves one of our greatest natural resources: our nation's farmland. CRP offers numerous upsides, such as the reduction of water runoff and sedimentation. Thereby offering heightened protection to our groundwater, lakes, rivers, ponds, and streams. The program is certainly favorable for our country's wildlife, as millions of acres of tillable land are set aside, allowing for ground cover establishment that serves as a welcomed habitat for wildlife. It also can have an appreciable impact on the backbone of this great country, the American farmer. By taking tillable land out of production that was once used to grow crops such as corn, soybeans, and wheat, CRP helps to keep the bottom from falling out of grain commodity prices.

Of course, like many other forms of governmental assistance programs, CRP also carries within it the potential for abuse. On a practical level, one of the unfavorable aspects of the well-intended program is that it issues payments to landowners for NOT working the land. This goes against the scriptures that unite monetary payout and commends (and rewards) hard work. Scripture examples such as:

> *For even when we were with you, this we commanded you, that*
> *if any would not work, neither should he eat. For we hear that*

there are some which walk among you disorderly, working not at all, but are busybodies. Now them that are such we command and exhort by our Lord Jesus Christ, that with quietness they work, and eat their own bread. (2 Thessalonians 3:10-12)

There is the CRP for America's farmers and landowners, and it has many merits as well as some shortcomings; but no such program exists within the framework of God's economy.

If we refuse to roll up our sleeves and answer the call or go about our work in our field half-heartedly and lacking in zeal, then that too has its own "reward" of sorts. *I went by the field of the slothful . . . And, lo, it was all grown over with thorns, and nettles had covered the face thereof, and the stone wall thereof was broken down.* (Proverbs 24:30-31) We are called to diligently work in our field as long as we live. *In the sweat of thy face shalt thou eat bread, till thou return unto the ground.* (Genesis 3:19a) As an encouragement, I would remind you that with sweat and toil come the sweet rewards of laboring in obedience to God: *The sleep of a labouring man is sweet, whether he eat little or much.* (Ecclesiastes 5:12) You may have never woken up in the morning on a SleepNumber® bed, nor have a Tempur-Pedic® mattress in your master bedroom, but work your field just the same, Christian. Sleep well.

It's never too late to be who you might have been.
~George Eliot

*Even when opportunity knocks, a man still has
to get up off his seat and open the door.*
~Anonymous

*Many an opportunity is lost because a man is
out looking for four-leaf clovers.*
~Anonymous

Be life long or short, its completeness depends on what it was lived for.
~David Starr Jordan

CHAPTER #6

Pay for the Field

For which of you, intending to build a tower, sitteth not down first, and counteth the cost, whether he have sufficient to finish it? Lest haply, after he hath laid the foundation, and is not able to finish it, all that behold it begin to mock him, Saying, This man began to build, and was not able to finish. (Luke 14:28-30)

COUNT THE COSTS

North Korean government officials would have exercised much wisdom, had they taken this verse to heart before breaking ground on what Esquire magazine dubbed, *The Worst Building in the History of Mankind.* The Ryugyong Hotel (aka, the hotel of doom, the phantom hotel, the tower of terror, and a myriad of other unflattering synonyms) is a towering, empty concrete shell that was once intended for use as a hotel in Pyongyang, North Korea, the capitol and largest city in the country. It reaches a massive height of 105 stories (just five stories short of the former World Trade Center Towers one and two) and reportedly encompasses nearly 4,000,000 square feet-a staggering 90 acres under one roof. Architectural plans called for eight rotating floors and seven revolving restaurants, perched high above the gargantuan hotel's 3,000 plus vacant rooms.

All of this serves to make The Ryugyong the largest hotel in the world that you will likely never receive a wake-up call from the front desk in, order room service from, or so much as go for a ride on the elevator in. This is so for three reasons. First, vacation travel to communist North Korea is highly restricted. Hey, even if travel in and out of the country was unrestricted, let's be honest, few have North Korea in the line of sight for their next weekend getaway. Secondly, in an effort to keep costs in check, suspect concrete was reported to have been used, calling into scrutiny the safety and integrity of the overall structure. Lastly, construction that began on the pyramid-shaped hotel in 1987 abruptly stopped in 1992 and would lay dormant for the next nearly 16 years due to insufficient funds.

The estimated cost of the hotel back in the mid '80's represented about 2% of North Korea's entire Gross National Product (GNP). Seems a little lavish, especially for a city (and a country) that is not on anyone's short list for a road trip. Clearly, someone was more than a tad negligent in failing to sit down and count the cost. While construction has resumed in recent years, even so, "NSF" is stamped firmly on the permanent record of the Ryugyong Hotel.

NSF

NSF. Nuclear Scientific Foundation? How about National Securities and Financial? Hmm, maybe Navy Seaman First-Class? Perhaps it is texting lingo for, Not So Fast? NSF could be all of these things and more, but when these three letters are put together in succession, it has one universally understood interpretation: Non-Sufficient Funds. North Korea knows it. Those three letters might as well be rubber stamped diagonally in ninety-six point cherry red font across the front of every photo, postcard, or desktop wallpaper in existence of The Ryugyong Hotel. In a dismal effort to salve their conscience and to conceal the proverbial elephant in the room, for much of the last two decades,

North Korean officials have edited the phantom hotel out of their city skyline photos before publishing. This is much the equivalent as when my one year old daughter sat on my lap and placed her hands over her eyes, smugly confident that she was now cleverly concealed from view and that Daddy can no longer see her!

None of us want to fall into the NSF trap that North Korea did, as they failed to count the costs upfront; nor would it be honest for us to airbrush over the ruins of failed attempts, relationships, and a myriad of other empty endeavors from the landscape of our lives. So, what steps can we take to minimize the likelihood of having "NSF" stamped across the field of our dreams? We all are too keenly aware there are no guarantees in life, but there are those things we can do to ensure we have what it takes to not only buy the field but have the means to pay for it as well.

CASH OR CREDIT OR . . . ?

Google Checkout and PayPal have enjoyed revolutionary influence in online purchasing behaviors. Membership has its privileges at American Express, and who could argue that Visa is everywhere you want to be. But there are no electronic credit card swipe machines conveniently located nearby God's field for you, and neither is payment in the form of a personal check on the short list of legal tender. MasterCard's ad slogan rings true, *There are some things that money cannot buy; for everything else, there's MasterCard.* The field certainly falls into the category of things that money cannot buy, and while *Life takes Visa,* the procurement of your field most definitely does not.

Scripture reminds us of the certainty that there will be fields purchased, *And fields shall be bought in this land, whereof ye say, It is desolate without man or beast; it is given into the hand of the Chaldeans. Men shall buy fields for money.* (Jeremiah 32:43-44) But if it's not credit cards or cash, exactly what kind of currency puts a *SOLD* sticker triumphantly across the *For Sale By Owner* sign jutting out of your field? Just what *gladly accepted here* payment stickers grace its glass entrance doors? Matthew 13:44 gives us some profound insights to the answer to this question and the unconventional, and unconditional, medium of exchange that is required. *Again, the kingdom of heaven is like unto treasure hid in a field; the which when a man hath found, he hideth, and for joy thereof goeth and selleth all that he hath, and buyeth that field.* Let's dissect this verse into smaller parcels, for within it we have a template for anyone that is committed to buying and paying for the field.

Currency #1: Diligence

Matthew 13:44 is a fitting monument to the life's work of diligent hands. In the workplace, no character trait is more esteemed, or in shorter supply, than that of diligence. Diligence can always be found walking alongside the one dead-set on making a difference for others. Diligence is often the tipping point between excellence and mediocrity, success and failure, wealth and poverty, leading and following, thriving and surviving, NSF and paid-in-full.

There is a biblical law of sowing and reaping put forth in scripture.

> *Be not deceived; God is not mocked: for whatsoever a man soweth, that shall he also reap. For he that soweth to his flesh shall of the flesh reap corruption; but he that soweth to the Spirit shall of the Spirit reap life everlasting. And let us not be weary in well doing: for in due season we shall reap, if we faint not.* (Galatians 6:7-9)

For the diligent soul that time and again shakes off weariness in doing well, a beautiful, bountiful harvest awaits to be reaped. Concerning the yield of diligence, A.W. Tozer once remarked, *The result of diligence is a faith that is strong and willing to inherit the fulfillment of the promises of God.* The following are a few of the many other great and desirous things that diligence reaps in the Christian life.

→In due season diligence reaps FINANCIAL SECURITY.

He becometh poor that dealeth with a slack hand: but the hand of the diligent maketh rich. (Proverbs 10:4) Lasting financial security-everyone wants it and fancies such from the longest of distances, but only the diligent have the hope of ever knowing it up close and personal for themselves.

→In due season diligence reaps AUTHORITY.

The hand of the diligent shall bear rule: but the slothful shall be under tribute. (Proverbs 12:24) An industrious individual that steadily sticks to his work day in and day out will be held in honor and advance in positions of responsibility and authority. *And the man Jeroboam was a mighty man of valour: and Solomon seeing the young man that he was industrious, he made him ruler over all the charge of the house of Joseph.* (1 Kings 11:28) This principle rings true not only in this present life, but in the eternal life that is to come as well. *His lord said unto him, Well done, thou good and faithful servant: thou hast been faithful over a few things, I will make thee ruler over many things: enter thou into the joy of thy lord.* (Matthew 25:21) In sharp contrast to the reward of the diligent, Proverbs 10:8 informs us that the idle and indolent life will be marked by dependency upon others and servants to the wise in heart.

Referred to often as the *Prince of Preachers,* Charles Spurgeon was a Baptist Pastor from the late 19th century. In one of his many stirring literary works, *John Ploughman's Talk,* Spurgeon offers page after page of practical wisdom and insights, at times dripping with satire, including this little gem about the one who lacks diligence and is given over to laziness.

> *Every man ought to have patience and pity for poverty; but for laziness, a long whip, or a turn at the treadmill might be better. This would be healthy physic for all sluggards; but there is no chance of some of them getting their full dose of this medicine,*

for they were born with silver spoons in their mouths, and like spoons, they will scarce stir their own tea unless somebody lends them a hand. They are, as the old proverb says, "as lazy as Ludham's dog, that leaned his head against the wall to bark;" and, like lazy sheep, it is too much trouble for them to carry their own wool . . . a man who wastes his time and his strength in sloth offers himself to be a good target for the devil, who is a wonderfully good rifleman, and will riddle the idler with his shots; in other words, idle men tempt the devil to tempt them. He who plays when he should work, has an evil spirit to be his playmate; and he who neither works nor plays is a workshop for Satan. If the devil catch a man idle, he will set him to work, find him tools, and before long pay him wages . . . My advice to my boys has always been, get out of the sluggard's way, or you may catch his disease, and never rid of it. I am always afraid of learning the ways of the idle, and am very watchful to nip anything of the sort in the bud; for you know it is best to kill the lion while it is a cub.[3]

All of this is the self-created lot of the one that has succumbed to idleness. But to the one that is given to industry, in due season, their diligence will reap the desirable fruit of authority.

→In due season diligence reaps ABUNDANCE.

The soul of the sluggard desireth, and hath nothing: but the soul of the diligent shall be made fat. (Proverbs 13:4) "Fat" carries the idea of abounding in provisions, never lacking any good necessity, and always having more than enough. I believe in the motivating power of having

―――――――― ∿ ――――――――
Sitting around on our hands and daydreaming does nothing to conjoin the dreamer with her dream.
――――――――――――――――――

a dream, a vision for our life; but sitting around on our hands and daydreaming does nothing to conjoin the dreamer with her dream. It has been well said, *No dream ever comes true, until you wake up and go to work.* Wishful thinking is perhaps the poorest and most unprofitable of all substitutes for hard work, and yet so many seem quite content to make the trade-off. The sluggard is ever covetous of that which he does not have and envious of those who have it. Often he is unwilling to do anything of his own volition to actually roll up his sleeves, get to work, and go after it.

➔In due season diligence reaps SUCCESS.

He that diligently seeketh good procureth favour. (Proverbs 11:27) Motivational speaker Anthony Robbins succinctly put it as follows, *The meeting of preparation with opportunity generates the offspring we call luck.* Whatever name you want to give it, luck/chance/fortune always has and always will take up sides with the diligent. Diligent people time and again seem to be the luckiest souls on the face of the earth, but there is nothing lucky about their favorable situation that they have procured for themselves by much diligence.

➔In due season diligence reaps GRATEFULNESS.

The slothful man roasteth not that which he took in hunting: but the substance of a diligent man is precious. (Proverbs 12:27) A sure-fire way to let what you have slip through your hands is to allow a sense of entitlement to encroach into your thought-life and take up residency. Just as certain as slothfulness reaps an ungrateful spirit towards others around you, as well as towards God and His provisions, diligent men and women are full of gratitude and do not have the time nor any interest to muse on such unprofitable thinking.

81

→In due season diligence reaps SOUND THINKING.

The thoughts of the diligent tend only to plenteousness; but of every one that is hasty only to want. (Proverbs 21:5) While it may not be on the radar of the CDC, (Center for Disease Control and Prevention) procrastination, laziness, and an entitlement-driven, somebody-owes-me-something mentality have nearly reached epidemic status in today's culture. In sharp contrast, diligent people have sound thinking. When you strive in your daily life to cultivate diligence in all that you do, you will find a completely unexpected, but welcomed by-product. Namely, that your mind is much more creative, optimistic, and full of ideas and possibilities-all of which are enablers to having more than enough. God blesses and rewards our endeavors when we make our minds up to honor these biblical precepts.

→In due season diligence reaps ADVANCEMENT.

Seest thou a man diligent in his business? he shall stand before kings; he shall not stand before mean men. (Proverbs 22:9) *Mean men* is not a description for base, wicked men; but rather those that are common, ho-hum, run-of-the-mill, average type individuals. Sooner or later, but always in due season, the diligent man or woman finds his way up near the top.

Those that are slothful have unwittingly enslaved themselves to the ball of regret and the chain of all that might have been in their lives.

In the feeblest of schemes to get noticed, those that are slothful have unwittingly enslaved themselves to the ball of regret and the chain of all that might have been in their lives. Diligence in your labor calls to mind your name to the attention of people that are in positions of power. If unconvinced, check out the biblical accounts of Joseph, Jeroboam, and Daniel to name but a few such diligent folks in scripture and the advancement that came their way as a result.

Diligence is a powerful, universally accepted form of currency, and with an eye towards the future it will literally take you anywhere you want to be. When buying the field, don't leave home without it.

The Currency of Discernment
The which, when a man hath found . . .

Do you recall from your childhood years, playing the game, *Hot-Warm-Cold?* It is sort of an inanimate twist on the classic, Hide-n-Go-Seek. One person simply hides an object and then calls for the other person to come and try to, as we say in the country, birddog it. As a help in tracking the item down, the one who hid the object will give the person clues of a thermal nature as to their closeness to finding the hidden object. For instance, if the person was not anywhere in close proximity to the object, the other might say, *You're cold. Freezing cold. You're like ice!* Then as the person made their way in the direction that they should go, they might hear counsel such as, *You're getting warmer. Warmer. Warmer. Hot. You're getting hot. You're burning up! Dude, you're like on fire!* I am sure the game has its variations from one part of the country to the next, but you get the gist.

One of the funny and frequent aspects of the game is when someone who is "on fire" is standing right by that which they are looking for, and yet they fail to see it. If they were any closer it would reach out and bite them, and they still cannot seem to spot it. Similarly, one of the frequent, but not nearly so knee-slapping funny aspects to life, is when someone is so very close to living the life they imagined for God's glory. They are within such proximity to unearthing God's calling upon their life, and yet, because of a lack in discernment, they fail to discover it. Three principal reasons could be cited as to why we come up short in the discernment department and miss those God appointed opportunities to buy the field.

1) <u>We are only looking for fireworks.</u>

I live in a small, rural town in the Midwest. We have two small grocery stores in our farming community, neither of which are national chains. One store is locally owned and operated by a friend who was a classmate of mine all the way through school, from the first day of Kindergarten to the time honored tradition of Senior Skip day. He married his high school sweetheart and the unassuming name of their piece of the American dream is "Bob's Food Mart." (And no, his name is not Bob) The other grocery store is part of a regional franchise, and like the good folks over at Bob's, they too are friendly, down-to-earth, hometown kind of people, and I suppose I know most everyone that works at each store on a first name basis, as many do me.

Collectively, both stores could tout about the same retail footprint as the floral department of the large supermarket stores found in most any major city across America. I know this for I spent nearly twenty years living in the great towns of Houston, Kansas City, Columbus, Ann Arbor and Indianapolis. I have a fond recollection of the days of walking into a Hen House, Randall's, Kroger or a Marsh store and be pleasantly confronted with some dear soul by the end cap on aisle 2 who wants me to sample a new flavor of chip dip. Over in the freezer section, I am almost accosted to nibble on a chicken cordon bleu entrée, already cut up in bite sized pieces, conveniently held together by a toothpick and served on a napkin resting comfortably on a silver platter. I comply with their wishes, but the taste from the first bite was indistinct as, like a dog gulping down a piece of raw meat tossed from his owner's hand, I swallowed the thing whole. A second cause could have been that delicious residue coating my taste buds from the sampling of a honey walnut cream cheese smeared on top of a cinnamon raisin bagel over in the dairy aisle that I was hesitant to confess to you. So, I clear my palette and have a second go at it, and yep, my initial gut instincts were confirmed-Yummy!

Walking down the freezer section in aisle 17, while heading to the check-outs, I am all but held at gun point to taste a new rising crust pizza, available in cheese lovers, pepperoni and supreme. By now I am so stuffed that I can hardly even walk. Every step is laborious, and just a few appetizers ago, I had to ask one of my kids to go and get Daddy one of those motorized cart thingies up at the front of the store that seem to be all the rage these days. Yet, I can see in his eyes that he can't bear the thought of another rejection, and so somehow, someway, from somewhere deep within, I take one for the team and savor a sample of each variety and grab a couple for the road (for the children).

The preceding account of my trip to the grocery store is offered tongue in cheek, but without any sort of justified basis, or historical, biblical, or even common sense precedent, we can unfairly expect opportunities to be presented in much the same manner as the described supermarket experience. We anticipate destiny to be vying for our eye-level attention and every turn and for fate to be served up hot and fresh on a silver platter almost everywhere that we are. Such opportunities rarely, if ever, garner our attention while heralded like a large banner in tow from a twin engine Cessna over our personal airspace.

There are exceptions of course, as the Old Testament describes one account of just how blatantly obvious the Lord was leading and guiding His children from Egypt to the promise land.

> *And the LORD went before them by day in a pillar of a cloud, to lead them the way; and by night in a pillar of fire, to give them light; to go by day and night: He took not away the pillar of the cloud by day, nor the pillar of fire by night, from before the people.* (Exodus 13:21-22)

I suppose even today, there are those rarest of Christian men and women who could give a testimony that God clearly spoke to them in a "burning bush" type manner. Praise God when He chooses to do such, but most of us would bear witness that God guides us and opens up doors of opportunity to buy and pay for the field, in a far more subtle, less obvious fashion. Someone noted, *Opportunities? They are all around us. There is power lying latent everywhere waiting for the observant eye to discover it.* While there are noteworthy exceptions, the complete absence of fanfare is likewise the prominent pattern from scripture of how God leads and guides. Consider these proof points.

> *I will instruct thee and teach thee in the way which thou shalt go: I will guide thee with mine eye.* (Psalms 32:8)

> *Trust in the LORD with all thine heart; and lean not unto thine own understanding. In all thy ways acknowledge him, and he shall direct thy paths.* (Proverbs 3:5-6)

> *And, behold, the LORD passed by, and a great and strong wind rent the mountains, and brake in pieces the rocks before the LORD; but the LORD was not in the wind: and after the wind an earthquake; but the LORD was not in the earthquake: And after the earthquake a fire; but the LORD was not in the fire: and after the fire a still small voice. And it was so, when Elijah heard it, that he wrapped his face in his mantle, and went out, and stood in the entering in of the cave. And, behold, there came a voice unto him, and said, What doest thou here, Elijah?* (1 Kings 19:11-13)

Opportunities to buy the field are all around us. But you'll miss it altogether if you expect it to show up at your doorstep dressed in an evening gown decked out with excessive bling and other flashy accessories amidst fanfare, paparazzi in tow or exploding fireworks. No, opportunity almost always makes her presence quietly known alongside us in the routine of everyday life inconspicuously dressed in khaki's and a button-down shirt.

2) <u>We fail to ask.</u>

Of all the regrettable reasons to let an opportunity slip through the cracks of our life, this perhaps is the most tragic. What a simply bonehead reason to be negligent towards a God-appointed opportunity. Scripture pretty much has my back on this one, too.

> *Ye lust, and have not: ye kill, and desire to have, and cannot obtain: ye fight and war, yet ye have not, because ye ask not.* (James 4:3)

> *If any of you lack wisdom, let him ask of God, that giveth to all men liberally, and upbraideth not; and it shall be given him.* (James 1:5)

You're roughly half way through the reading of this book; if you haven't already taken a pause along the way to ask God for discernment concerning His field for you, now would be a good time to set the book aside for a few moments and do exactly that. Such was the first thing that a young lady named Achsah did, as she was about to start a new life with Othniel. Scripture records that she approached her father Caleb and asked him for a field. *And it came to pass, as she came unto him, that she moved him to ask of her father a field: and she lighted off her ass; and Caleb said unto her, What wouldest thou?* (Joshua 15:18) When was the last time you posed the same question to your Father? God invites you to do just that. *Thus saith the LORD the maker thereof, the LORD that formed it, to establish it; the LORD is his name; Call unto me, and I will answer thee, and shew thee great and mighty things, which thou knowest not.* (Jeremiah 33:2-3) From His throne of grace, our heavenly father stands at the ready, saying to His children, "What wouldest thou?"

3) <u>We are entirely too busy.</u>

One of the prevailing evils of our day that is largely undetected is this matter of busyness. Somewhere along the way, far too many have bought the lie hook, line, and sinker, that busyness equates to productiveness. That busy people are productive people, successful people, happy people, fulfilled people. Yet in most cases, the correlation is conspicuously absent. Two solemn accounts from scripture come readily to mind, the first being that of Martha. She had the opportunity of a lifetime to enjoy close fellowship with Jesus personally, live and in the flesh; and yet in her busyness, the opportunity was squandered. Another lady named Mary had a to-do list that was every bit as long, and yet she resisted the impulse to be hurried and plopped herself down at the feet of her Lord.

> *Now it came to pass, as they went, that he entered into a certain village: and a certain woman named Martha received him into her house. And she had a sister called Mary, which also sat at Jesus' feet, and heard his word. But Martha was cumbered about much serving, and came to him, and said, Lord, dost thou not care that my sister hath left me to serve alone? bid her therefore that she help me. And Jesus answered and said unto her, Martha, Martha, thou art careful and troubled about many things: But one thing is needful: and Mary hath chosen that good part, which shall not be taken away from her. (Luke 10:38-42).*

In our own busyness, by default we unknowingly make far more decisions for ourselves (and for others closest to us) than we could ever imagine. A second of many cautionary reminders of the remorseful byproduct of busyness is set before us in the book of 1 Kings.

> *And as the king passed by, he cried unto the king: and he said, Thy servant went out into the midst of the battle; and, behold, a man turned aside, and brought a man unto me, and said, Keep this man: if by any means he be missing, then shall thy life be for his life, or else thou shalt pay a talent of silver. And as thy servant was busy here and there, he was gone. And the king of Israel said*

unto him, So shall thy judgment be; thyself hast decided it. (1 Kings 20:39-40)

Some reading this are perhaps old enough to remember the movie, *The African Queen*, based on the book by author, C.S. Forester. In his book, the author describes at some length the dilapidated old steamboat for which the movie is named. He depicts the laborious exertions required of the skipper just to get up a sufficient head of steam to get her under way. The trouble was that there were so many leaks, so many faulty seams and joints, that the power was dissipating into thin air and only with the greatest of difficulty could the old boat be persuaded to muster up a fraction of her original power. Its force was diluted by the not so dynamic duo of erosion and neglect. The steam oozed out in all kinds of futile ways, instead of being channeled to thrust with single-minded purpose.

What time and neglect did to the physical make-up of the steamboat, rendering her largely useless, is much like the prolonged effect that a lifetime of busyness has on us spiritually. Busyness serves to do not only its sinister work of wearing us down and out, it also keeps us distracted so that we are completely blinded to some amazing opportunities that God has for us. If I could pen I Kings 20:40 in the shadow of this truth, it would read something like, *And as the well intentioned Christian was busy here and there, the opportunity was gone.*

The Currency of Delight
And for the joy thereof . . .

We can do a lot of right things but not necessarily with the right spirit or fueled by the right motivation. Stepping out in faith and buying the field is an awesome, most worthwhile adventure for us to devote ourselves to. But if we do so with an embittered or resentful spirit, or for any other aim than giving Christ the glory due His name, then the blessing is forfeited.

As a marked difference to the faith of the first century church, Christianity today often comes across as a joyless faith. The same that was said of Cain could be likewise said of too many Christians today, *And Cain was very wroth, and his countenance fell. And the LORD said unto Cain, Why art thou wroth? and why is thy countenance fallen?* (Genesis 4:5-6) Falling stock prices and home values are often in the news, but not once has falling countenances of Christians everywhere been flashed on a ticker across the bottom of a television screen during the evening newscast. We are long overdue to remember that, *the joy of the Lord is your strength* (Nehemiah 8:10) and beg God with the prayer, *The LORD lift up his countenance upon thee, and give thee peace.* (Numbers 6:26) We could cry out as David did, *Restore unto me the joy of thy salvation; and uphold me with thy free spirit.* (Psalm 51:12) This new and unimproved, joyless genre of Christianity today is doing its level best in making us weary and taking its toll on our strength.

If our joyless countenance could be mistaken for the mug shot of Cain, then we need to ask God to help the visage that others see in us more closely resemble the joyful countenance of Caleb. *But my servant Caleb, because he had another spirit with him, and hath followed me fully, him will I bring into the land whereinto he went; and his seed shall possess it.* (Numbers 14:24) The different spirit of Caleb was certainly one chiefly marked by faith, but I believe that springing from that faith there was a joy that resonated brightly from Caleb's countenance, the kind of joy that was evident in his life as a young man, all the way up through his twilight years.

> *Forty years old was I when Moses the servant of the LORD sent me from Kadeshbarnea to espy out the land; and I brought him word again as it was in mine heart. Nevertheless my brethren that went up with me made the heart of the people melt: but I wholly followed the LORD my God. And Moses sware on that day, saying, Surely the land whereon thy feet have trodden shall be thine inheritance, and thy children's for ever, because thou hast wholly followed the*

LORD my God. And now, behold, the LORD hath kept me alive, as he said, these forty and five years, even since the LORD spake this word unto Moses, while the children of Israel wandered in the wilderness: and now, lo, I am this day fourscore and five years old. As yet I am as strong this day as I was in the day that Moses sent me: as my strength was then, even so is my strength now, for war, both to go out, and to come in. Now therefore give me this mountain, whereof the LORD spake in that day; for thou heardest in that day how the Anakims were there, and that the cities were great and fenced: if so be the LORD will be with me, then I shall be able to drive them out, as the LORD said. (Joshua 14:7-12)

I offer this poem which cites the courageous words of Caleb, a joyful, decisive hero of the faith, when he declared to Joshua, *Now therefore give me this mountain.* (Joshua 14:12) May we too implore the court of Heaven with the mantra, *Give me this field!*

Give Me This Mountain (by Shirlee Kimball)

Give me this mountain today, dear Lord; even the peaks so high;
Let me lift up mine eyes to the distant hills, as the end of the day draws nigh.

If I linger too long in the valley, dear Lord, I might lose the will to go on; For each hour of the day that I do not climb, makes the journey seem harder and long.

Give me this mountain today, dear Lord, while the soft breezes blow o'er my soul;
while the sunlight gleams on the distant hills, and I can still clearly see my goal.

*Give me this mountain today, dear Lord; it's a stepping stone to
eternal day;*
*One more mountain, one more hill, Lord; one more step on
life's way.*

The Currency of Dedication
Goeth and selleth all that he hath . . .

Paul is a shining example of dedication and single-mindedness in devotion to the cause of Christ that is sorely needed today.

> *Not as though I had already attained, either were already perfect:*
> *but I follow after, if that I may apprehend that for which also I*
> *am apprehended of Christ Jesus. Brethren, I count not myself to*
> *have apprehended: but this one thing I do, forgetting those things*
> *which are behind, and reaching forth unto those things which are*
> *before, I press toward the mark for the prize of the high calling of*
> *God in Christ Jesus.* (Philippians 3:12-14)

In the spirit of full disclosure, I must confess that I have not been totally upfront. Amidst the rally cries, the incessant pleading, and the unrelenting solicitation to buy the field, I have been less than forthcoming in one fundamental truth that you have every right to know. For some time now, I have been wrestling with trying to figure out how to best go about breaking the news. The proverbial elephant in the room that can be ignored no longer is the answer to the question, "What is the asking price of the field?"

I can almost hear it now, "Fine, I am going to need discernment, delight, and a healthy dose of diligence, but how much of this dedication thing am I going to have to cough up? I mean, what is the field even listed for sale at anyway? Exactly how much is all of this going to set me back?" These are all fair questions and you have been more than patient.

So here goes. The non-negotiable list price is (drum roll please) . . . The Owner's firm asking price is set at (take a deep breath) . . . The amount someone must give in exchange for the field is (one last pause for effect) . . . EVERYTHING. Be mindful that it was said of the man in our Lord's parable that for him to buy the field he must, *selleth all that he hath.* Friend, it will be no different for you or for me. Think about it, if you or I were able to buy the field for anything less than our "all," the individual in Matthew 13:44 would then have a pretty solid case for price discrimination.

While "all" is pretty straightforward and easily defined, from person to person and field to field, it can morph a bit. Here are a handful of testimonies of what "all" looked like to a few men and women in scripture that bought the field.

It cost a poor widow all her livelihood.

And Jesus sat over against the treasury, and beheld how the people cast money into the treasury: and many that were rich cast in much. And there came a certain poor widow, and she threw in two mites, which make a farthing. And he called unto him his disciples, and saith unto them, Verily I say unto you, That this poor widow hath cast more in, than all they which have cast into the treasury: For all they did cast in of their abundance; but she of her want did cast in all that she had, even all her living. (Mark 12:41-44)

It cost Paul all that he had once held so dear.

But what things were gain to me, those I counted loss for Christ. Yea doubtless, and I count all things but loss for the excellency of the knowledge of Christ Jesus my Lord: for whom I have suffered the loss of all things, and do count them but dung, that I may win Christ. (Philippians 3:7-8)

It cost Moses all his family ties and riches.

By faith Moses, when he was come to years, refused to be called the son of Pharaoh's daughter; Choosing rather to suffer affliction with the people of God, than to enjoy the pleasures of sin for a season; Esteeming the reproach of Christ greater riches than the treasures in Egypt: for he had respect unto the recompence of the reward. (Hebrews 11:24-26)

It cost all of the disciples their career paths.

And when they had brought their ships to land, they forsook all, and followed him. (Luke 5:11)

It cost another woman all of her life savings.

And being in Bethany in the house of Simon the leper, as he sat at meat, there came a woman having an alabaster box of ointment of spikenard very precious; and she brake the box, and poured it on his head. (Mark 14:3)

Don't ever forget that buying His Father's field cost Jesus His life.

Even as the Son of man came not to be ministered unto, but to minister, and to give his life a ransom for many. (Matthew 20:28)

And as Christians, you and I are not exempt from paying the price to follow Christ. *Verily, verily, I say unto you, The servant is not greater than his lord; neither he that is sent greater than he that sent him.* (John 13:16)

Chalk it up to inflation, supply and demand, or more accurately, the unchanging ways of God, but field listing prices have not decreased any since the accounts of these men and women from the Bible. But know that when we devotedly pledge our all to the cause of Christ, we are promised a return on our investment that is beyond measure and makes your and my finite "all" seem pale when compared alongside of God's infinite "all."

> *Then Peter said, Lo, we have left all, and followed thee. And he said unto them, Verily I say unto you, There is no man that hath left house, or parents, or brethren, or wife, or children, for the kingdom of God's sake, Who shall not receive manifold more in this present time, and in the world to come life everlasting.* (Luke 18:28-30)

The Currency of Decisiveness

Re-read Matthew 13:44. For the remainder of days, may we never again read through Matthew's gospel and look at this one verse quite the same. Notice the complete absence of hesitation. Observe that there is not even so much as a hint of waffling or procrastination. *Procrastination is the natural assassin of opportunity* and there is an atmosphere of decisiveness which permeates this account and so very much of the scriptures. That same decisiveness was present when Jesus was calling His disciples. One day he was walking along the shore of the Sea of Galilee and saw brothers Peter and Andrew out casting their nets while fishing.

Procrastination is the natural assassin of opportunity

> *And he saith unto them, Follow me, and I will make you fishers of men. And they straightway left their nets, and followed him.*

And going on from thence, he saw other two brethren, James the son of Zebedee, and John his brother, in a ship with Zebedee their father, mending their nets; and he called them. And they immediately left the ship and their father, and followed him. (Matthew 4:19-22)

Prayer, fasting and the acquiring of wise counsel are indispensable in the Christian's life. Untold disappointments stemming from innumerable bad decisions could have been side-stepped had we sought after and heeded to godly counsel and spent time with the Lord seeking His face on the matter. That said, much of the time the issue in our lives is not that we are uncertain what God would have us to do; rather the issue rests in whether or not we are willing to obey that which He has commanded. Missionary to the Philippines, Bob Hughes once said, *Why do you need a call, when you have a command?* Oh, for a prevailing attitude of decisiveness to obey, when the Lord clearly reveals glimpses of His will upon our hearts. Would to God, we would beg Him for the courage, and a mustard seed faith to seize opportunities from Him.

Why do you need a call, when you have a command?

The expression "window of opportunity" is not just trite, overused business vernacular, but rather has utility for individuals, churches, parenting and relationships. There is even a window of opportunity concerning salvation, *Seek ye the LORD while he may be found, call ye upon him while he is near.* (Isaiah 55:6) *For he saith, I have heard thee in a time accepted, and in the day of salvation have I succoured thee: behold, now is the accepted time; behold, now is the day of salvation.* (2 Corinthians 6:2) An Eastern proverb gives a sobering reminder of the penalty assessed for indecision and missed opportunities, *Four things come not back: The*

Would to God, we would beg Him for the courage, and a mustard seed faith to seize opportunities from Him.

---

spoken word, The sped arrow, The past life, and The neglected opportunity. Each day is a once in a lifetime opportunity. Don't miss your window today.

WHAT'S IN YOUR WALLET

Diligence. Discernment. Dedication. Delight. Decisiveness. All are non-negotiable tender necessary to buy the field, and all five represent very different forms of currencies indeed. In fact, we could say that they are so different than which we are accustomed, that they are "foreign" currencies. Not foreign in the sense of some distant land far from home, but foreign in the sense of altogether uncommon, largely unknown or unheard of. And as a "foreign" currency, it should be noted:

1) We must give something of equal value in exchange to procure them.
2) The exchange rate on these currencies does not fluctuate; it is always high, for they never trade "weak" or lose their value.
3) These unique currencies can only be found in and extracted from the wallet of faith.

Unfortunately these currencies, like the $2 bill, have largely gone out of circulation and are about as rare to find as a buffalo nickel or an Indian head penny. What's the reason for such scarcity? To exchange them, these foreign currencies all require a prevailing element of faith. To Christians, we are most thankful for faith when it exerts itself as a noun. A noun faith is a saving faith, and we praise the Lord that salvation is by faith, *For by grace are ye saved through faith.* (Ephesians 2:8) But there is another side to faith, and while we have an unbecoming tendency to consolidate the two, the reality is faith also can take on a distinct verb-like persona as in, *The just shall live by faith.* (Romans 1:17) So then, faith is not just something that is a one-time necessity on the day of salvation. Rather, it is a daily requirement for serving God and living a life that is pleasing to Him.

If given the option, most will take a first round bye on a faith that serves God; a faith that stretches us; a faith that we are not only saved by, but must also live our life daily by. And yet, every enduring work that has ever been undertaken for the glory of God had as its point of origin a Holy Spirit implanted burden in the heart of men. In order for such a work to make the transformation from a burden within one's heart to that of a blessing in the lives of others, there is the necessity of faith.

> Every enduring work that has ever been undertaken for the glory of God had as its point of origin a Holy Spirit implanted burden in the heart of men.

More than twenty years prior to my enrolling in Bible College, I was a student at a state college in Missouri where my roommates and most of my close friends were aviation majors, all studying to be commercial airline pilots. There are many sequential ratings, or certifications, that pilots must obtain before they can ever fly commercially. Flight ratings such as student, sport, multi-engine, recreational, private and instrumentation are sequential prerequisites which line the path leading to Captain-hood.

The instrumentation rating is somewhat unique and is the next certification to master after one achieves their initial private rating. Such check rides take place not in the openness of daytime but in the cover of darkness with an instructor pilot. This is so because the pilot in training is flying not by sight but rather exclusively by the readings on the plane's instrumentation. Of course there is a whole world of discovery and adventure and soaring to new heights which awaits the pilot beyond that of their instrumentation rating. But the point is, none of that will ever be experienced until the pilot first learns to trust his instrument reads and flies not by sight, but rather by faith in the direction that the gauges on his instrumentation panel instruct him in.

And so it is for the Christian. After being saved by faith, the next sequential prerequisite on the checklist is this matter of learning to trust God and to live by faith, *For we walk by faith, not by sight.* (2 Corinthians 5:7) There is a whole other world awaiting the Christian-a world of discovery, adventure and the attainment of new heights. None of that is going to come to pass, however, until we first obtain our spiritual instrumentation rating and once and for all learn to trust the leading of the Holy Spirit in our lives and walk by faith. We may well have a home reserved in Heaven, but until we pass this test we are like the grounded 747 out on the tarmac citing mechanical issues. Might as well ask the stewardess if she knows where you can score a Snickers bar, because we aren't going anywhere soon. *But without faith it is impossible to please him: for he that cometh to God must believe that he is, and that he is a rewarder of them that diligently seek him.* (Hebrews 11:6) Jesus Christ's return is near and He is looking for Christians to step out in faith and buy the field. Scripture poses the arresting question that every Christian needs to take to heart. *I tell you that he will avenge them speedily. Nevertheless when the Son of man cometh, shall he find faith on the earth?* (Luke 18:8) Now knowing the type of "currency" that is required to buy the field, what's in your wallet?

Even if you're on the right track, you'll get run over if you just sit there.
~Will Rogers

Opportunities always look bigger going than coming.
~Anonymous

If you don't risk anything, you risk even more.
~Erica Jong

Death is more universal than life; everyone dies but not everyone lives.
~A. Sachs

CHAPTER #7

Stay in the Field

Go not to glean in another field, neither go from hence, but abide here. (Ruth 2:8)

I THINK I CAN, I THINK I CAN

You've grown up with the story and even read it to children. It is a legendary tale of determinism, optimism, and old fashioned let's roll up our sleeves and get'r' done. A little railroad engine (the runt of the litter type) was employed at a station yard for pulling a few cars on and off the tracks. Then one fateful morning the call came in as a long train of freight-cars needed to be pulled up and over a steep hill. One by one, much larger train engines were tasked to fill the work order. The excuses came rolling in, *I can't; that is too much a pull for me*, said one engine. One by one, they all refused to pull the load. Last on the list, the little switch engine was asked if he would be willing to pull the load up the grade and down on the other side. The faith filled response from the littlest train in the station yard that day was, *I think I can*. The little locomotive then put itself in front of the heavy load that was so despised by his beefier peers and began to tug. At first, it was inch by inch, but then he began to build a little momentum as the little engine kept bravely puffing faster and faster, all the while declaring to himself, *I think I can, I think I can, I think I can.*

As he neared the top of the hill, which had so intimidated the larger engines, the little train went much more slowly, but still kept saying all the way up, *I—think—I—can, I—think—I—can.* And drawing from all available resources and mustering every last bit of courage and strength, it did just that. Then the little engine that could went on down the other side of the grade, beaming with pride all the while proudly whistling, *I thought I could, I thought I could.*

THE EARLY BIRD GETS SOMETHING WAY BETTER THAN A SLIMY WORM

It was a beautiful spring day in May of 1990 in the city of Cleveland, Ohio, for the start of the Revco-Cleveland Marathon. For those more serious enthusiasts who desire to run the entirety of the marathon, they are to be at the starting line first. For those more recreational runners wanting to run "just" 10k, they are to line up behind the others. Ms. Johnson, a 42 year old secretary, showed up for the race intending to take part in the 10k that she had trained for but ended up running the full marathon. According to the Associated Press, *Runner Georgene Johnson got to the starting line fifteen minutes early. The mistake cost her 20 miles and aching knees, but she said she's proud of the foul-up.*[1]

She realized her error when she and four thousand or so other runners left the downtown area and headed towards the suburbs. Fortunately, around mile seven or eight, Georgene came up alongside a helpful runner with some seemingly good advice, which was in essence; slow down, pace yourself, and once you make it to the halfway point you can catch a courtesy shuttle vehicle back to the starting line.

But when she did reach the halfway mark, to her surprise, Georgene was feeling pretty good. Way better than she expected, and so she carried on. *I got to mile 20 and it was like, well, I only have 10K left*, she told the *Times*. Her finishing time was 4:04, despite never having run more than eight miles in her life! Amidst pushing herself forward at the steepest part of her twenty-six mile "hill," she adopted the, *I think I can! I think I can!* mental fortitude, as perspiration streamed from the pores of her sweat glands mile by grueling mile. Georgene had every sort of temptation to quit at each arduous checkpoint along the way, and no one would have faulted her in the least for having done so. But then again, no one would still be telling her incredible story to this day if she would have.

For every single right contributor to stay in your field, there are dozens of regrettable causes to up and quit. The world is full of quitters. After years of daily, highly regimented practice, many have perfected the not so fine art of throwing in the towel. Most of us have a long, rich legacy of starting things, but when things begin to go off-script, and the race is proving to be a lot more drawn out and difficult than envisioned, we fail to finish. The fifth chapter of Romans tells us that sin is hereditary. *For as by one man's disobedience many were made sinners.* (Romans 5:19) In much the same manner as we all inherited our sin gene from Adam, somewhere along the way there spawned a quitter's gene, and unlike hemophilia and color blindness, this gene doesn't skip a generation. Everyone is susceptible to yield and many do succumb to the impulse to quit.

The quitter's gene may be hereditary, but your succumbing to it is not. I'd like to propose a few of the top reasons why those who go to great lengths to consider, buy, and work the field, don't always stay in the field and finish their course. But it is not enough to just identify the problem; we will then counter that with the remedy for us to stay.

One cause for quitting is so predominant, namely the discouragement which stems from barrenness, the lack of visible indicators that our labors are making a difference, that we will deal with it singularly in the following chapter.

Reason #1 To Quit the Field: *We take our eyes off Christ.*

The famed author and Nobel Prize winner Alexander Solzhenitsyn spent part of his life in a Soviet Siberian prison. At one point he was so physically weak and discouraged that he hoped for death. The hard labor, terrible conditions and inhumane treatment had taken its toll. He knew the guards would beat him severely and probably kill him if he stopped working, so he planned to expedite his death by simply ceasing his work and then leaning on his shovel. When he stopped, a fellow, caring Christian reached over with his shovel and quickly drew a cross in the sand at the feet of Solzhenitsyn. Then just as quickly erased it before the guard could see what had been drawn. Solzhenitsyn would later record that his entire being was energized by that little reminder of the hope and courage found in Christ. He found the strength to continue because a friend cared enough to remind him to cast his eyes afresh on the hope that is Christ.

Remedy to Overcome the Temptation to Quit:

Looking unto Jesus the author and finisher of our faith; who for the joy that was set before him endured the cross, despising the shame, and is set down at the right hand of the throne of God. For consider him that endured such contradiction of sinners against himself, lest ye be wearied and faint in your minds. (Hebrews 12:2-3)

Reason #2 To Quit the Field: *We focus on ourselves.*

With our eyes no longer affixed on Christ, our line of sight will naturally meander somewhere towards something else or someone else, and hey, what better person than ourselves! This has proven many times over to be an influential cause in the life of the average quitter. Our stumbles, let downs, disappointments, and failures are magnified exponentially when filtered through the easily wounded lens of self. We become disheartened and the next thing you know, we are hanging out in Quittersville. I am not talking about a drive-by, just in town for the weekend, or even a snowbird-type getaway for a couple months out of the year, either. Rather a known-by-all, full-fledged fixture, property-tax-paying resident in this densely populated, homogenous community of fellow quitters.

> Our stumbles, let downs, disappointments, and failures are magnified exponentially when filtered through the easily wounded lens of self.

Remedy to Overcome the Temptation to Quit:

Let nothing be done through strife or vainglory; but in lowliness of mind let each esteem other better than themselves. Look not every man on his own things, but every man also on the things of others. (Philippians 2:3-4)

Reason #3 To Quit the Field: *We are transient and soft.*

When we get to heaven, after the Judgment Seat of Christ, subsequent to a reunion with others who have gone before, and following the marriage supper of the lamb, if such is at all possible, I think there is going to be some serious ribbing taking place around the water cooler of heaven. The saints of old are going to be having some fun at the expense of us 21st century saints. They are going to let us have it about how easy we had it compared to them (you know, the proverbial, they had to walk in a blinding snowstorm to and from school uphill, both ways, in two feet of freezing snow). And I, for one, will probably have to tip my hat in respectful acceptance of their claim as if to say, you're right. Kudos. Point well taken. Chalk one up for the old timers. Well played, sirs.

Our quest for a painless life of comfort and ease has stripped us of our energy and stamina to stick it out. We don't approach our assignment with the necessary mental toughness necessary for tenure. We have become transient, borderline nomadic, lacking a long term come what may—I'm here to stay, mindset. When the going gets tough; we get going . . . going, gone.

> Our quest for a painless life of comfort and ease has stripped us of our energy and stamina to stick it out.

Many Christians can pack it up and call it a day faster than summertime swimmers can exit a public pool following the lifeguard's whistle at the first sound of distant thunder.

Just like the dear soul that gets woozy and passes out at the sight of blood, we get lightheaded and faint at the mere thought of having to endure some hardship, trial, or time of testing. *If thou faint in the day of adversity, thy strength is small.* (Proverbs 24:10) Yet for reasons known only to Him, on occasion it pleases God to have His children go back for second helpings of a plateful of adversity. *And though the Lord give you the bread of adversity, and the water of affliction.* (Isaiah 30:20a) Directly or indirectly, such return trips to the "buffeting buffet" can most always be sourced back to God.

The following tell-tale signs of physical softness equates quite directly to the spiritual softness of Christianity today. These are actual comments which were supposedly left on Canadian Provincial Park registration sheets and comment cards by backpackers completing wilderness camping trips.

→*Trails need to be reconstructed. Please avoid building trails that go uphill.*

→*Too many bugs, leeches, spiders, and spider webs. Please spray the wilderness to get rid of these pests.*

→*Please pave the trails. Chair lifts need to be in some places so that we can get to wonderful views without having to hike to them.*

→*The coyotes made too much noise last night and kept me awake. Please eradicate these annoying animals.*

→*A small deer came into my camp and stole my jar of pickles. Can I get reimbursed? Please call . . .*

→*Escalators would help on steep uphill sections.*

→*A McDonald's would be nice at the trailhead.*

→*Too many rocks in the mountains.*[2]

These complaints in the suggestion box indicate that the people who made them fail to truly grasp what it means to stay for a night or two roughing it in a wilderness area. They were looking for something convenient and comfortable, not a true wilderness experience. In a similar way, when we mumble and grumble and are ready to throw in the towel, it is yet another indicator that we have lost sight that the Christian is not called to live life down at the community rec center but out on the battlefield, and that Heaven is there, not here.

Remedy to Overcome the Temptation to Quit:

Thou therefore endure hardness, as a good soldier of Jesus Christ.
No man that warreth entangleth himself with the affairs of this
life; that he may please him who hath chosen him to be a soldier.
(2 Timothy 2:3-4)

Reason #4 To Quit the Field: *We are Covetous.*

A chief hindrance to not staying in our field is that we find ourselves fantasizing about what it must be like in the enviable field of another. We covet the look, feel, size, location, newness, notoriety, or size of someone else's. *And they covet fields, and take them by violence; and houses, and take them away: so they oppress a man and his house, even a man and his heritage.* (Micah 2:2) If you think about it, almost every sin affecting society can be traced back to covetousness, or idolatry as the Bible calls it. St. Louis may be known as the gateway to the west and marijuana is sometimes referred to as a gateway drug, but covetousness is truly the gateway sin.

Immediately after Jesus instructs Peter to feed His sheep, Christ tells Peter that he (Peter) will die for the faith. Peter's not so crazy about his life forecast; the news of his demise out on the field of faith. So, he looks over and spots John; *Peter seeing him saith to Jesus, Lord, and what shall this man do? Jesus saith unto him, If I will that he tarry till I come, what is that to thee? follow thou me.* (John 21:21-22) In other words, Peter cries out to Jesus, "What about Johnny boy? Yeah, what about him over in the corner? What exactly is the fate of the great beloved one and HIS field?" Jesus said in effect, "Peter, that's not your concern. Don't burden yourself with such thoughts. You just focus on following me." Come to think of it, that is probably pretty good advice for you and me as well.

<u>Remedy to Overcome the Temptation to Quit:</u>

Neither shalt thou desire thy neighbour's wife, neither shalt thou covet thy neighbour's house, his field. (Deuteronomy 5:21a)

Reason #5 To Quit the Field: *Rear-View Mirror Glances.*

It only stands to reason, that when we are looking back, we are going to make an absolute train wreck of things in any attempt to move forward. Scripture attests, *A double minded man is unstable in all his ways.* (James 1:8) Everyone knows that Mom has eyes in the back of her head, but for the rest of us we can only glance in one direction at a time and make any forward progress. Rear-view mirrors are handy when affixed to the windshield of a car; but they serve only to cripple and hamstring forward momentum when they dangle down from the mental recesses of our minds. What a cumbersome, ill-advised way to go through life, being guided by what your mind's eye recalls.

> When we are looking back, we are going to make an absolute train wreck of things in any attempt to move forward. Rear-view mirrors are handy when affixed to the windshield, but they serve only to hamstring forward momentum when they dangle down from the mental recesses of our minds.

The decision to look back was disastrous for Lot's wife, *But his wife looked back from behind him, and she became a pillar of salt.* (Genesis 19:26) In the end tally of things, it will be no more advantageous for us. *And Jesus said unto him, No man, having put his hand to plough and looking back, is fit for the kingdom of God.* (Luke 9:62)

<u>Remedy to Overcome the Temptation to Quit:</u>

Let thine eyes look right on, and let thine eyelids look straight before thee . . . Turn not to the right hand nor to the left. (Proverbs 4:25, 27)

ALL SALES FINAL

I was out shopping for a gift for my wife in a small, privately owned clothing store in a nearby town where they were having a clearance sale. Upon entering the store, the first thing my eyes took note of was the huge sign which read, "Store Clearance-All Sales Final." I didn't give it much thought and walked on in, being greeted by the owner who is a neighbor of mine. (Yep, it's true-everyone pretty much knows everyone in a small town!)

As I was perusing the sale racks, I found a lovely ladies coat that I knew she would like, IF it was the right size. I took it over to the cash register and asked, "This is a gift for my wife. If it doesn't fit, can I bring it back?" I fully expected to hear something along the lines of, "Absolutely", as if the unmistakable "All Sales Final" sign greeting people as they entered the store was just for common folk and did not apply to a likeable neighbor such as myself. His unexpected response was sudden and clear, "No. All sales are final."

I stepped away from the counter and looked again at the coat and tried to picture my dear wife in it and how it would fit her. While the garment was discounted heavily, the price was still over one-hundred dollars and I was hesitant. After considering the purchase for a few moments, knowing fully that there were no refunds or exchanges, I bought the coat. The story has a happy ending, in that my wife loved it and it fit her perfectly!

In much the same manner, we need a generation of Christian men, women, and young people, who will step up and buy the field God has for them with the same kind of, "All Sales Final" fortitude. No returns. No exchanges. No regrets. No leaving. No looking back. No second-guessing.

Lester Roloff was a great preacher who went to be with the Lord in 1982. Others have stated, *When a brave man takes a stand, the spines of others are stiffened.* Such would certainly be true of Roloff. While he was one of the most influential preachers of his day, he also recorded a song that, in essence, is a challenge to stay in your field. Within its stanzas, Roloff relays the account of the boy David, who refused to run, and by faith, stood against a giant of a man.

> We need a generation of Christian men, women, and young people, who will step up and buy the field God has for them with the same kind of, "All Sales Final" fortitude.

Further into the song, Roloff implores us to refuse to bow, but instead take our stand, as did Shadrach, Meshach, and Abed-nego, knowing that the furnace thermostat would be placed on its highest setting. A third and last stanza serves as an inspiration to dare to be a Daniel and to not bow down or back away, even when we know the lions in their den are licking their lips. While most any junior high school language teacher might rightfully cringe at the following usage of grammar in the chorus, my heart leaps and is motivated all the more to stay in my field. How about you?

> *When a brave man takes a stand, the spines of others are stiffened.*

Run if you want to run if you will cuz I came here to stay.

If I fall down, gonna get a right up cuz I didn't start out to play.

Its a battlefield brother, not a recreation room, Its a fight and not a game.

Run if you want to, run if you will, but I came here to stay.

111

PART III

Finishing God's Call

You may be disappointed if you fail, but you are doomed if you don't try.
~Beverly Sills

*It is often hard to distinguish between the hard
knocks in life and those of opportunity.*
~Frederick Philipse

*Success is a journey, not a destination. The doing is
often more important than the outcome.*
~Arthur Ashe

Luck is what happens when preparation meets opportunity.
~Lucius Annaeus Seneca

*Those who dream by day are cognizant of many things
which escape those who dream only by night.*
~Edgar Allen

CHAPTER #8

When the Field is Barren

Although the fig tree shall not blossom, neither shall fruit be in the vines; the labour of the olive shall fail, and the fields shall yield no meat; the flock shall be cut off from the fold, and there shall be no herd in the stalls: Yet I will rejoice in the LORD, I will joy in the God of my salvation. (Habakkuk 3:17-18)

BARREN MISSION FIELDS

Regardless of the desired "crop" that was to have grown, barren fields are heartbreakingly discouraging. Perhaps none more so than a barren mission field. Many names are well recognized for the impact on the foreign mission field. But few realize that most "successful" missionaries went through seasons of despondent barrenness. Let me share with you two such testimonies—the first from a missionary to India, and the second, a missionary to South Africa.

William Carey, often called the father of modern missions, arrived in India in 1793 with a burden to preach the Gospel of Jesus Christ to those who had never heard His name. For seven years he proclaimed the Gospel message faithfully week after week, month after month, year after year. The end result of close to a decade of prayer, preaching, witnessing and Christian service found Carey with not so much as a single convert to Christ, despite all his faithful labors.

Carey could easily have grown discouraged and allowed himself to return home defeated and empty-handed, but he had faith that in God's time, He would bless and the barren field would be bountiful. To his sisters back home in England Carey wrote this letter.

> *I feel as a farmer does about his crop: sometimes I think the seed is springing, and thus I hope; a little blasts all, and my hopes are gone like a cloud. They were only weeds which appeared; or if a little corn sprung up, it quickly dies, being either choked with weeds, or parched up by the sun of persecution. Yet I still hope in God, and will go forth in His strength, and make mention of His righteousness, even of His only.*[1]

A second testimony would be that of Robert and Mary Moffat. They labored faithfully in Bechuanaland (present day Republic of Botswana, located in South Africa) without so much as a ray of encouragement to brighten their way. After an entire decade of service, they could not report a single convert from all of their untiring efforts. Finally, the directors of their mission board began to question the wisdom of continuing the work. The thought of leaving their post brought great grief to this devoted couple, for they felt sure that God was in their labors and that they would see people turn to Christ in due season.

They stayed, and for a year or two longer it was more of the same. Nothing. Only prolonged, excruciating barrenness. Then one day a friend in England sent word to the Moffats that she wanted to mail them a gift and asked what would be a blessing to them. Trusting that in time the Lord would begin to move and bless their work, Mrs. Moffat replied, *Send us a communion set; I am sure it will soon be needed.*

God honored that dear woman's faith, in the midst of a bleak and barren field. The Holy Spirit did indeed move upon the hearts of the villagers and soon a little group of six converts were united to form the first church in that land. The communion set from England was delayed in the mail; but on the very day before the first commemoration of the Lord's Supper in Bechuanaland, the set arrived!

By faith, Carey fought off the overwhelming sense of discouragement and kept working tirelessly in his barren field. He would go on to establish what many would say is the greatest work in the history of modern day missions. It was not by sight, but by faith, that the Moffats did much the same thing. Now it is our turn. It is our turn to work the field even when, especially when, all that is visible is barren.

> *I would seek unto God, and unto God would I commit my cause: Which doeth great things and unsearchable; marvellous things without number: Who giveth rain upon the earth, and sendeth waters upon the fields.* (Job 5:8-10)

May we, like Job, realize that only God can send the rain of His blessings upon desolate works and barren fields; and let us be content to work in those fields until He does.

LAMBSQUARTER AND ROOTWORMS

Growing up on a row crop and cattle farm in the Midwest, there was only one focus in the spring and that was getting the crops in to the field. The preparatory work of spring planting might actually begin as early as the prior fall. Once the previous crop was harvested, soil nutrients such as anhydrous ammonia could be worked in the soil to give a nitrogen boost to plants the following spring. With the arrival of spring, of course there was much more work done to the soil with a plow, disc, harrow, and when that was all finished, a planter. Times have changed, but back in those days, Dad might even have one of his three sons go out into a field and hand-pull rogue weeds that managed to break through, despite our best efforts to prevent them.

My Dad was a good farmer. A fellow could search his whole life and not find a more hard-working individual. He was a man who not only had the physical strength to put in long hours of intensely manual labor but also the mental wherewithal to grow great yielding crops. Some seasons, he enjoyed "bumper crops" from out of the fields. But not every year. The Bible speaks of an ebb-and-flow; a season to all of life. *To every thing there is a season, and a time to every purpose under the heaven . . . a time to plant, and a time to pluck up that which is planted . . . A time to get, and a time to lose . . . What profit hath he that worketh in that wherein he laboureth?* (Ecclesiastes 3:1-2, 6, 9) And there were definitely those times growing up on the farm where, despite the most diligent of human efforts, there was a crop failure and a resulting barren field.

The causes for barrenness were numerous-Too much rain; too little rain. The temperatures were too hot, withering the plants before their fruit could bloom; or the weather was too cool, and soil temperatures not warm enough for crop seeds to germinate. There were other lurking factors as well. Weeds such as lambsquarter, milkweed and giant foxtail crowded out soybeans. Insect pests such as European Corn Borers would eat away at the ears of corn, while corn rootworms would chomp away at the root system of the plant. Every farmer then and now would freely confess that in the successful crop equation, there are many elements in the mix that are simply beyond his control.

Scripture attests to this truth as well. The book of Deuteronomy, speaks to the inevitability of factors largely outside of man's control, *Thou shalt carry much seed out into the field, and shalt gather but little in; for the locust shall consume it.* (Deuteronomy 28:38) Ecclesiastes is a book of man's wisdom written by the wisest man to ever live, Solomon. In one verse in chapter nine, he implores us to give our very best effort in all that we do, and in the next verse issues the reminder that, despite the most tireless of efforts, there are those times where one's best simply falls short.

Whatsoever thy hand findeth to do, do it with thy might; for there is no work, nor device, nor knowledge, nor wisdom, in the grave, whither thou goest. I returned, and saw under the sun, that the race is not to the swift, nor the battle to the strong, neither yet bread to the wise, nor yet riches to men of understanding, nor yet favour to men of skill; but time and chance happeneth to them all. (Ecclesiastes 9:10-11)

Along with death, the one paramount fear we all share is that of failure. It is no respecter of gender, age, wealth, appearance or any other demographic. Some toss and turn in their beds losing sleep over this fear and are even plagued with reoccurring nightmares. Just the thought of it can elevate our heart rate and bring on clammy hands, as beads of perspiration begin to dot across our worried and anxious foreheads.

Some of us have positions and/or are involved in ventures where we can conceal or mask failure longer than others. For row crop farmers, however, there is nowhere to run or hide. Even the lay person who can't tell the difference between a cutworm and a dung beetle can do a drive by at 55 MPH on a gorgeous summer day and tell at a casual glance if a field is experiencing crop failure or not. Barren fields know no disguise.

Despite the most carefully thought out plans and diligent labor, eventually we are all likely to experience up close and personal a season of barrenness in our life's work. Here are five helpful areas to immerse ourselves in when we find ourselves in the grips of such barrenness.

1) <u>Pray That You Will Not Lose Heart</u>

Discouragement is the tried and true tactic of the enemy. *And they journeyed from mount Hor by the way of the Red sea, to compass the land of Edom: and the soul of the people was much discouraged because of the way.* (Numbers 21:4)

From the launching pad of a discouraged heart, things quickly went from bad to worse for God's people. In verse five we see that they begin to be critical to authority and their leadership. *And the people spake against God, and against Moses, Wherefore have ye brought us up out of Egypt to die in the wilderness? for there is no bread, neither is there any water; and our soul loatheth this light bread.* All of this culminating in the death of many people in verse six, *And the LORD sent fiery serpents among the people, and they bit the people; and much people of Israel died.* Don't overlook the fact that a loss of heart was the ball that got things rolling in the wrong direction. Discouragement setting in the hearts of God's people became ground zero for the destruction that would follow.

The people were following Moses who was doing his best to follow God. In route to the promise land, they were going the way they believed God would have for them and yet, amidst the barrenness of the wilderness which surrounded them, discouragement encroached and settled in even to their very soul.

I am mindful of the Bible truth affirmed for us in Proverbs 13:15 that, *the way of transgressors is hard.* But if we are completely transparent, many could also say that there are those seasons of life when the way of the Christian is hard, too. In such times, if we are not very careful and deliberate in protecting our spirit and in the guarding of our heart, then discouragement barges in like an uninvited wedding guest, grabs some punch and props his feet up as the first of many lamentable dominoes begin to fall in our lives. Missionary to abandoned children in India, Amy Carmichael, once said, *Everywhere the perpetual endeavour of the enemy of the soul is discouragement. If he can get the soul under the weather, he wins.* Don't let him win, Christian.

Everywhere the perpetual endeavour of the enemy of the soul is discouragement. If he can get the soul under the weather, he wins.

---

2) **Stick to Your Work**

Whether the field is bountiful or barren-stick to the work. It is not our part, nor wholly within our power, to be successful; only faithful. Richard Cecil once was quoted as having said:

> *Some men will follow Christ on certain conditions-if He will not lead them through rough roads-if He will not enjoin them any painful tasks—if the sun and wind do not annoy them—if He will remit a part of His plan and order. But the true Christian, who has the spirit of Jesus, will say, as Ruth said to Naomi, "Whither thou goest I will go," whatever difficulties and dangers may be in the way.*[2]

Our motivation to serve God in His field must be for His glory, and out of a faithful heart of willing obedience, knowing that, *All things work together for good to them that love God, to them who are the called according to his purpose.* (Romans 8:28)

> It is not our part, nor wholly within our power, to be successful; only faithful.

If two men ever had a seemingly just cause to throw in the towel and quit the work, it would have been Abraham Lincoln here in the United States and William Wilberforce in England. Lincoln's story of moving from one failure to another until he finally reached the office of the Presidency is astounding and looks something like the following:[3]

1832	Lost his job
1832	Defeated running for state legislature
1833	Failed business endeavor
1835	Sweetheart died
1837	Suffered a nervous breakdown
1838	Defeated for Speaker
1843	Defeated for nomination to Congress

1848	Lost re-nomination
1849	Rejected for Land Officer
1854	Defeated for U.S. Senate
1856	Defeated for Vice-President
1858	Defeated again for U.S. Senate
1860	Elected President of the United States

Perhaps Lincoln was encouraged to continue on because of one man's testimony from the other side of the pond more than a half century prior. Let me share with you a portion of Wilberforce's story and his incredible resolve to finish what he started.

William Wilberforce was a British politician in the late 1700s who championed the causes of human rights and civility across the globe. He began his political career as an independent Member of Parliament for Yorkshire in 1780. In many respects, he was a typical British politician of his time. There was nothing special or spectacular about his work in London. But during his early days as a statesman, he came to know Christ as his Savior, and subsequently his outlook on life and work in politics changed. Dramatically.

Stemming from his newfound Christian faith and keen sense of morality, Wilberforce led campaigns for causes such as the Society for Suppression of Vice, British missionary work in India, the creation of a free colony in Sierra Leone, the foundation of the Church Mission Society, and the Society for the Prevention of Cruelty to Animals. Wilberforce's most noted work began in 1787 when he was approached by Granville Sharp, Hannah More, and Charles Middleton. These three were activists who petitioned hard against the slave trade of England, and seeing the injustice in such acts, Wilberforce agreed to join with them and head the parliamentary campaign against the British slave trade.

For twenty-six years, Wilberforce tirelessly fought in the parliament to end Britain's involvement in the wicked practice. At times he felt he would never see it through to victory, yet he stuck to his work, played thru the pain, and continued on in the fight to the finish. In 1833 as Wilberforce lay on his death bed, the British Parliament passed the Slavery Abolition Act 1833, which abolished slavery in most of the British Empire. Three days later, William Wilberforce died.

For over a quarter of a century, Wilberforce worked hard to end slavery in Great Britain. Can you imagine the opposition he faced and the trials he endured those twenty-six years? At one point, he so wished to quit, believing success would be forever elusive. It was then that his friend (and former slave trader) John Newton sent him a note to encourage him in finishing his life's calling. And finish he did. Let the following words of encouragement from an anonymous writer serve as a rally cry for our hearts as well, that we might also stay in the field and finish our life's calling.

> *Keep about your work. Do not flinch because the lion roars; do not stop to stone the devil's dogs; do not fool away your time chasing the devil's rabbits . . . let the devil do his work; but see to it that nothing hinders you from fulfilling the work God has given you . . . Keep about your work . . . until at last you can say, "I have finished the work which Thou gavest me to do."*

Christian friend: Don't flinch. Stick to your work.

3) <u>Know that God Has a Plan, Even When We Don't Understand It.</u>

The account is told of a discouraged Pastor who had the following strange dream. He was standing on the top of a great granite rock, trying to break it with a pick-ax. Hour after hour he worked with no result. No yielding of the rock to his blows. At the point of exhaustion, he said, *It is useless; I will stop.* Suddenly a man stood by him who had been watching his labors and asked: *Were you not allotted this task? And if so, why are you going to abandon it? My work is vain; I can make no impression on the granite,* said the discouraged Christian. Then the stranger solemnly replied, *That is not your task; your duty is to pick, whether the rock yields way or not. The work is yours; the results are in other hands. Work on. Work the work.*

While God always rewards those who faithfully serve Him in His field, He seldom does so in our timing and in a manner that we would have scripted for ourselves. Sometimes, even, the reward tarries until we reach Heaven. When we cannot be shaken

> *The work is yours; the results are in other hands. Work on. Work the work.*

from the knowledge that we are doing His will and yet it is only barrenness which we have to show for our efforts, we have to remind ourselves that He is God and we are not. He is the Creator and we the creature. *For my thoughts are not your thoughts, neither are your ways my ways, saith the LORD. For as the heavens are higher than the earth, so are my ways higher than your ways, and my thoughts than your thoughts.* (Isaiah 55:8-9) He has the view from 30,000 feet up, while we are foot soldiers with a limited line of sight.

God has a plan behind the seeming failures in our lives, but we have to have faith that continues to serve amidst barrenness, as did missionaries William Carey and Robert & Mary Moffat. We must continue to have trust in Him and His ways, despite great heartache and unmentionable personal loss, as did Job. *Though he slay me, yet will I trust in him: but I will maintain mine own ways*

> Opportunity often arrives on the scene, fashionably late and appearing altogether different than we had been anticipating and praying for.

before him. (Job 13:15) God has a Divine plan for setbacks and in the wake of such events, opportunity often arrives on the scene, fashionably late and appearing altogether different than we had been anticipating and praying for.

Illustrative of this truth, a successful businessman was growing old and knew the time to choose a successor had arrived. Instead of selecting one of his directors, or even one of his children, he was determined to do something different. As the story is told, he called all the young executives in his company together as the following account transpires.

It is time for me to step down and choose the next CEO. I have decided to choose one of you. I am going to give each one of you a seed today—One very special seed. I want you to plant the seed, water it, and come back here one year from today with what you have grown from the seed I have given you. I will then judge the plants that you bring, and the one I choose will be the next CEO.

One man named Jim was there that day and he, like the others, received a seed. He went home and excitedly told his wife of all that had taken place. She helped him get a pot, soil and compost, and he planted the seed. Every day, he would water it and watch to see if it had grown. Jim kept checking his seed, but nothing ever grew. Three weeks, four weeks, five weeks went by, still nothing. By now, others were talking about their plants, but Jim didn't have any such plant; nothing visible to show for all his best labor and efforts and he felt like a failure. A full six months went by—still nothing in Jim's pot of soil; fertilized and watered from his own sweat and tears. By this point, everyone else in the office was talking about their beautiful trees and tall plants, but he had nothing. For one entire year, Jim managed just to keep on doing what he thought was right; he kept watering and fertilizing the soil which housed the seed that he so wanted to see grow.

A year finally went by and all the young executives of the company brought their plants to the CEO for inspection. On the drive into work, Jim felt sick at his stomach; it was going to be the most embarrassing moment of life.

He took his empty pot to the board room. When Jim arrived, he was amazed at the variety of plants grown by the other executives. They were beautiful, and all shapes, sizes, and varieties of plant life graced the room. Jim put his empty pot on the floor, and many of his colleagues smirked and pointed, while others openly laughed him to scorn.

When the CEO arrived, he surveyed the room and greeted his young executives. Jim just tried to disappear in the back. *My, what great plants, trees, and even flowers you have grown*, said the CEO. *Today one of you will be appointed as the next Chief Executive Officer.* And then, the CEO spotted Jim at the back of the room with his empty pot. He ordered the financial director to bring him to the front. Jim was terrified. His mind raced with such thoughts like, *The CEO knows I'm a failure! Now everyone will know I am a failure. Maybe even, he will have me fire*d.

When Jim got to the front, the CEO asked everyone to sit down except Jim. He looked at Jim, and then announced to the young executives, *Behold your next Chief Executive. His name is Jim.* Jim couldn't believe it. He couldn't even grow his seed. *How could he be the new CEO*, the others said?

Then the CEO replied, *One year ago today, I gave everyone in this room a seed. I told you to take the seed, plant it, water it, and bring it back to me today. But I gave you all boiled seeds; they were dead—It was not possible for them to grow. All of you, except Jim, have brought me trees and plants and flowers. When you found that the seed would not grow, you substituted another seed for the one I gave you. Jim was the only one with the courage and honesty to bring me a pot with my seed in it. Therefore, he is the one who will be the new Chief Executive.*[4]

Odds are good that someone reading this has been tilling the soil of his field for a great deal longer than one year, with little visible results to show for it. Even the ten years of fruitlessness on behalf of the Moffets may seem like a blink of the eye when compared to how long you have been at your task. You don't know why it is, and neither do I, but don't overlook the mysterious ways of God. *For thus saith the LORD; Like as I have brought all this great evil upon this people, so will I bring upon them all the good that I have promised them. And fields shall be bought in this land.* (Jeremiah 32:42-43) We just need to understand that God has a plan, even though we often are not privy to fully understanding it.

4) <u>Rejoice in Him</u>

It will be worth our while to take a second glance at the text that graced the top of this chapter.

> *Although the fig tree shall not blossom, neither shall fruit be in the vines; the labour of the olive shall fail, and the fields shall yield no meat; the flock shall be cut off from the fold, and there shall be no herd in the stalls: Yet I will rejoice in the LORD, I will joy in the God of my salvation.* (Habakkuk 3:17-18)

Even though the stalls were empty, and no farm animal could be found grazing out in the fields, and harvest time was met only with failure, Habakkuk still rejoiced and provided us a template for what to do when our field reeks of barrenness. The words of the Psalmist advocate a similar plea, *Let the field be joyful, and all that is therein.* (Psalm 96:12)

I shared earlier an excerpt from one of Charles Spurgeon's books, "John Ploughman's Talk." Few are familiar with this particular literary work of his, but one that is more widely recognized and well-read is Spurgeon's daily devotional, "Morning and Evening." As the name implies, he penned two devotional thoughts for each day. The text for one such day's writing was Isaiah 54, and is titled, *SING, O BARREN ONE*; a humble call to rejoicing though surrounded by barrenness.

Sing, O barren, thou that didst not bear; break forth into singing, and cry aloud, thou that didst not travail with child: for more are the children of the desolate than the children of the married wife, saith the LORD. Enlarge the place of thy tent, and let them stretch forth the curtains of thine habitations: spare not, lengthen thy cords, and strengthen thy stakes; (Isaiah 54:1-2)

Although we may have brought forth some fruit and have a joyful hope that we are abiding in the vine, yet there are times when we feel very barren. Prayer is lifeless, love is cold, faith is weak, each grace in the garden of our heart languishes and droops. We are like flowers in the hot sun, desperately needing the refreshing shower. In such a condition what are we to do? The text is addressed to us in just such a state. "Sing, O barren one . . . break forth into singing and cry aloud." But what can I sing about? I cannot talk about the present, and even the past looks full of barrenness. I can sing of Jesus Christ. I can talk of visits that the Redeemer has paid to me in the past; or if not of these, I can magnify the great love with which He loved His people when He came from the heights of heaven for their redemption. I will go to the cross again. Come, my soul, you were once heavy-laden, and you lost your burden there. Go to Calvary again. Perhaps that very cross that gave you life may give you fruitfulness . . . Sing, believer, for it will cheer your own heart and the hearts of others who are desolate. Sing on, for although you are presently ashamed of being barren, you will be fruitful soon; now that God makes you hate to be without fruit He will soon cover you with clusters. The experience of our barrenness is painful, but the Lord's visits are delightful. A sense of our own poverty drives us to Christ, and that is where we need to be, for in Him our fruit is found.[5]

5) <u>Finish Your Course</u>

Lincoln and Wilberforce were more recent men who faced much opposition and failure, and had every cause to quit. But in the Bible, no man ever had such numerous reasons to quit than the Apostle Paul. And yet, he refused to yield to such enticement. At the end of his Christ-centered life, listening for the loathsome steps of the executioner from the confines of a dark, lonely Roman prison cell, Paul was able in good conscience to write these final words for our betterment, *I have fought a good fight, I have finished my course, I have kept the faith.* (2 Timothy 4:7) Of course Paul's motivation and example was Christ, who said, *I have glorified thee on the earth: I have finished the work which thou gavest me to do.* (John 17:4) Jesus Christ must be our Supreme example and His life the pattern for ours as well. Why are we mindful to be Christ-like in so many needful areas of our Christian walk but often negligent in this important matter of being like Jesus in our resolve to finish our course?

BOOSTER SHOTS FOR DISCOURAGED HEARTS BEATING IN BARREN FIELDS

A booster shot is the periodical administering of an additional medicine to give a needed lift or "boost" to one's immune system. There are booster shots available for a variety of vaccines and I can confidently tell you that spiritual booster shots need to be administered much more frequently than the recommended ten year schedule for tetanus and diphtheria. While I am not in the field of medicine, from the field of "been there, done that, got the miserable T-shirt," let me share with you three booster shots. Perhaps these will give a lift to the downcast heart and increase the Christian's immunity to the dreaded disease of discouragement.

Courage Booster Shot#1: Look Up

Looking unto Jesus the author and finisher of our faith; who for the joy that was set before him endured the cross, despising the shame, and is set down at the right hand of the throne of God. For consider him that endured such contradiction of sinners against himself, lest ye be wearied and faint in your minds. Ye have not yet resisted unto blood, striving against sin. (Hebrews 12:2-4)

That is exactly what David did when he and his men returned home to Ziklag and they were surrounded by barrenness. Unbeknownst to them, just prior to their arrival home, the Amalekites had rode into town and taken all of the women and children captive. Then, from one city limit sign to the other, they proceeded to burn the place down the ground.

This was not the homecoming reception that David and his men had fancied. I can only imagine the jaw-dropping speechlessness there must have been that day in Ziklag, as the men looked at the destruction and were anxious to know the welfare of their wives and children. Then the emotional rollercoaster ride began, and the speechlessness gave way to a state of shock and then to mourning, and ultimately to anger, as all eyes shifted towards David and someone from deep within the angry mob yelled, "Get a rope!" Scripture picks it up from here.

> *And David was greatly distressed; for the people spake of stoning him, because the soul of all the people was grieved, every man for his sons and for his daughters: but David encouraged himself in the LORD his God.* (1 Samuel 30:6)

David was on the receiving end of the original "if looks could kill" gaze from those around him. So what did he do? He looked upward and, *encouraged himself in the Lord.*

God has wired us for the mutual giving and receiving of encouragement from others around us. *Iron sharpeneth iron; so a man sharpeneth the countenance of his friend.* (Proverbs 27:17) That's the way it should be. That's God's plan. But each of us are painfully aware that things don't always go to plan. Ultimately, every Christian is responsible for the overall health of his or her Christian walk, and there are those times when a Barnabas, whose name means, *son of consolation*, is nowhere to be found on the landscape of our lives. In such times, if we are to go on for God and not quit, the onus is on us to be found *Looking unto Jesus* and *consider him* as we encourage ourselves in the Lord our God.

Courage Booster Shot #2: Look Around

Therefore seeing we have this ministry, as we have received mercy, we faint not. (2 Corinthians 4:10)

When our lives are engulfed with barrenness, we need to remember that we have been given a ministry and keep our hearts encouraged to follow and fulfill that ministry. *And say to Archippus, Take heed to the ministry which thou hast received in the Lord, that thou fulfil it.* (Colossians 4:17) We have a success-oriented mindset here in America, and allow that thinking to drift over into ministry and into the church. When we don't see "success"-when there is barrenness, we lose heart and sight of God's calling for us.

One of the most influential preachers in America today is Dr. Paul Chappell, who is the pastor at Lancaster Baptist Church in Lancaster, California. I really like what he has said concerning the success syndrome in Christian work. *Ministry is not about fulfilling the "American Dream". It is about fulfilling the calling of God.* Remember that Christian and take heart. God has not called you to be successful in the eyes of others; rather to be faithful in His eyes.

Courage Booster Shot #3: Look Ahead

And Gideon came to Jordan, and passed over, he, and the three hundred men that were with him, faint, yet pursuing them. (Judges 8:4)

Just two chapters prior in Judges 6:11, we see Gideon in a valley threshing wheat, hiding out from the Midianites. *And there came an angel of the LORD, and sat under an oak which was in Ophrah, that pertained unto Joash the Abiezrite: and his son Gideon threshed wheat by the winepress, to hide it from the Midianites.* Threshing wheat was a work to be done out in the open, up on a hilltop even, so as to take advantage of the wind to blow the chaff away from the wheat kernels. But we see him down in the valley by the winepress because every time he and every other Israelite threshed wheat out in the field, the Midianites came along and snatched it from them. *And Israel was greatly impoverished because of the Midianites.* (Judges 6:6)

Again and again, Gideon sees all that he has worked for out in the field pass right through his hands and into the hands of another. Amidst the barrenness, Gideon feels defeated and discouraged. He has lost all confidence in, and the vision for, God's calling on his life. If only I were a wagering man, I would be willing to bet my bottom dollar that Gideon was so discouraged that he was to the point of being ready to hoist the white flag high and flat out quit. But he didn't. Don't miss that. He pressed on and in so doing, you and I look back and remember Gideon today in the same light that God viewed him even when he was playing the role of the coward, as scripture records, *And the angel of the LORD appeared unto him, and said unto him, The LORD is with thee, thou mighty man of valour.* (Judges 6:12)

Hey, it's super easy to get discouraged when the field is barren, and to then be searching high and low for a way out. But being called as a co-laborer into God's field was never about taking the easy path, but rather all about following the right path and staying on it. So when things in your life are not going to plan, and all the happenings around you are very much off script and despair encroaches upon your spirit, cry out to God as did the Psalmist. *My flesh and my heart faileth: but God is the strength of my heart, and my portion for ever.* (Psalm 73:26) And let us heed the counsel from scripture to, *let not your hearts faint, fear not, and do not tremble, neither be ye terrified because of them; For the LORD your God is he that goeth with you, to fight for you against your enemies, to save you.* (Deuteronomy 20:3-4)

FINISH IT

By 7 p.m. on October 20, 1968, at the Mexico City Olympics Stadium, the sun was beginning to set and the skies darken. High temperatures from earlier in the day had cooled down, as the last of the Olympic marathon runners crossed the line and were being assisted by team doctors, coaches, team-mates, family and friends. Over an hour earlier, Mamo

---
Rest assured, God is a Finisher.

Wolde of Ethiopia had charged across the finish line, winning the twenty-six mile long race, looking nearly as strong and vigorous as when he'd started.

While the last few thousand spectators were making their way to the exits, they heard police sirens and whistles through one of the gates which entered the stadium. All attention was now focused on that gate, where a sole figure sporting the distinctive green and blue colors of the United Republic of Tanzania came limping into the stadium. His name was John Steven Aquari. He was the last man to finish the marathon in 1968, as his leg was bandaged and bloody from a bad fall he had taken early in the race. Now, it was all he could do to limp his way around the track, as the remnant of an earlier, much larger crowd stood to their feet and applauded while he completed that last lap of his race.

When he finally crossed the finish line, having completed his race, many approached and gathered around him. One man dared to ask the question that all were tempted to. *You are badly injured. Why didn't you quit? How come you didn't you just give up?* Bruised and battered, a resolved Aquari said with quiet dignity, *My country did not send me seven thousand miles to start this race. My country sent me to finish.*

So it is with God. God didn't call us just to start some great work out in the field; He would have us to finish that which He laid upon our heart to begin. Rest assured, God is a Finisher. I think it would please Him for us to do the same. As Christians, we have all the resources of heaven to do so and be the finishers God would have for us to be. *Being confident of this very thing, that he which hath begun a good work in you will perform it until the day of Jesus Christ.* (Philippians 1:6) Like the bruised and battered runner proudly wearing the colors of Tanzania all the way to the finish line, let us proudly wear the banner of our Lord out into the field and, whether bountiful or barren, stay in the field.

------------------ ∿ ------------------

As Christians, we have all the resources of heaven to do so and be the finishers God would have for us to be.

And let us not be weary in well doing: for in due season we shall reap, if we faint not. (Galatians 6:9) Discouraged? Perhaps. Feeling as though you are about to faint? At times, yes. Ready to quit? No way. Not on your life.

Our deepest fear is not that we are inadequate. Our deepest fear is that we are powerful beyond measure. It is our light, not our darkness, that frightens us most . . . We were born to make manifest the glory of God that is within us. And when we let our own light shine, we unconsciously give other people permission to do the same. As we are liberated from our own fear, our presence automatically liberates others.
~Marianne Williamson

Opportunity is often missed because we are broadcasting when we should be tuning in.
~Anonymous

Opportunity knocked. My doorman threw him out.
~Adrienne Gisoff

Let us strive on to finish the work we are in . . .
~Abraham Lincoln

CHAPTER #9

Lost Yield of the Field

The field is wasted, the land mourneth . . . Be ye ashamed . . .
because the harvest of the field is perished. (Joel 1:10-11)

"UN"MADE IN CHINA

*L*ong since abandoned "ghost towns" from the days of the wild, wild, west blanket sections across the southwestern United States. Places such as old gun slingin' towns in Kansas like Whiskey Point, or St. Elmo further out west in Colorado. Golden State towns such as Bodie and Calico, that reached their zenith during the great California gold rush. Heading over to Arizona, you will not find any place more deserted or entrenched with the lore that was the old west, than the area which surrounds Tombstone.

However, not every such town had to drop their city limit sign to "zero" as a result of the end of the gold rush or with the cessation of the great era that was the railroad. Towns that could be right out of the movie "Cars," such as Glenrio, New Mexico or Two Guns, Arizona were once vibrant communities and centers of much activity and commerce along the famed Route 66. The cause of death of these communities and countless others just like them? The advent of the interstate. I-40 to put a name with the face.

The uninhabited ruins of such towns have become faded monuments to the glory that once was. As with any descent from former heights, it is sobering to see the decrepit state of such things today in contrast with the glory of what they were. But some remnant of comfort, however small, rests in the knowledge that at least these towns once had their "day in the sun." In spite of their present day obscurity and dilapidation, such locales did in fact reach their potential before being cut off at the knees by four lanes of asphalt. At least someone somewhere has some fond recollections and maybe even a few old photos tucked away in a shoebox from the "good ol' days."

But what about those towns and, more personally, what about those people, who never did peak? What about all the unrealized plans where no memories or photos exist, because despite amazing potential and wonderful opportunities, there was a failure to launch?

Enter Wonderland-the most amazing theme park that you will never go for a ride on the log flume in, have your picture taken with Wonderland characters, or cough up $9 for a hamburger over lunch. But you will find three hundred acres of half completed buildings, parking lots, and the steel skeletons of rides of what could have been, should have been and might have been but was not. Located a short drive north of Beijing, China, Wonderland was slated to be the biggest theme park in all of Asia. But in 1998, two years into full-scale construction, land agreements between the developer and surrounding farmers hit an insurmountable snag, as they could not come to terms on a price for the adjacent fields. Since that time no progress has been made and for all the years to come, it is pretty much shaping up much the same way at Wonderland. Nada. Looks like no ride on the teacups for you.

Go ahead and do an image search on the web for "China Wonderland" and you will scarcely believe your eyes. The photos conjure images in one's mind of a post-apocalyptic downtown Disney, complete with a Cinderella-like haunted castle as its centerpiece, surrounded by hundreds of acres of cornfields and shattered dreams.

The root cause of this epic failure lies in what I have been describing throughout this entire writing. While it feels more than a little presumptuous to try and arm-chair Quarterback the whole sordid thing from half a world away, the layman's response to the sad turn of events is that someone did not count the cost and in the end was unwilling to buy the field. Literally. So now, the field is wasted, marked only by departed joy and ruin. *For the fields of Heshbon languish . . . And gladness is taken away, and joy out of the plentiful field.* (Isaiah 16:8, 10) The series of unfortunate events at Wonderland resulting in it lying in ruin is a travesty, but when much the same thing happens in the lives of God's people, it is a tragedy.

LIFE ON CANNERY ROW

Cannery Row (first published in 1945), is a novel written by American author John Steinbeck. Henri is one of Steinbeck's characters in this book, and he's known for the unique boats he constructs with such detail and intricacy that it often takes years to work on just one. But there's more about Henri than meets the eye. With all of his well-laid plans, painstaking efforts, and years of experience in boat construction, he has yet to finish a boat. Not a single, solitary one. Each and every time, when the vessel is almost to the point of completion, he takes the boat entirely apart and starts all over again. Despite the pretense, Henri has no intention of ever actually placing the boat in the water and setting sail. Two of his friends discuss his peculiar, but by now, predictable behavior:

> *Every time he gets it nearly finished, he changes it and starts all over again. I think he's nuts. Seven years on a boat!" "You don't understand. Henri loves boats, but he's afraid of the ocean. He likes boats, but supposed he finishes his boat. Once it's finished people will say, 'Why don't you put it in the water?' Then if he*

puts it in the water, he'll have to go out in it and he hates the water. So you see, he never finishes the boat—so he doesn't ever have to launch it.[1]

Cannery Row has been classified under the genre of fiction, but it surely possesses a very non-fiction feel to it, for isn't that what happens with so many of our dreams? We make plans and tinker around with them for years, with little to no intention of ever actually finishing them. Fear mounts and with it, the risk of failure. The uncertainty of it all simply feels too great, and so we eek out some meager existence and timidly make our way through everyday life, playing things much further on the safe side than God ever intended us to.

Rather than dealing with our fear of the water and ultimately our fear of failure, we go through the motions of working on "boats" that we have no intention of ever finishing and placing in the water. As others have aptly put forth, *Ships are safe in the harbor; but then again, that's not what ships were made for.*

What's the "boat" you have been puttering around with? What has been your excuse for not finishing it? Let me see if I can put to good use my superhuman powers of mind-reading and take a stab at what some of those excuses might be: *I've been busy. I don't have the time. Someone else could do it better. What if I fail? I just can't. I'm afraid.* When our personal space feels violated and our toes get stepped on a bit, we have a saying out here in the country that resonates, *Am I plowing too close to the corn?*

I have a hunch these are your excuses, not because of any superhuman powers but because of my own personal experiences of making similar rationalizations. Your excuses have been my excuses, and it's time to stop saying, *I can't* and start saying, *By God's grace, I can.* It's time to stop making excuses and start making time. Finish the boat, take it down to the water's edge, do as Jesus instructed His disciples

> It's time to stop making excuses and start making time.

in Luke 5, *launch out into the deep,* and see what happens next. Maybe the thing will float. Maybe instead it will sink straight to the bottom. Either way, let's get it out of the, *I'm gonna' someday* mire of procrastination and get it out on the water. Who knows what God just might do with it, if we would just let go of the fear and release it from our hands, entrusting it into His.

REGRETS ONLY

According to author Tony Campolo, in his book, *Who Switched the Price Tags,* fifty people over ninety-five years old were asked one question: *If you could live your life over again, what would you do differently?* Of course many different answers were received, but three common responses to the repeatedly surfaced. People said that they would:

1. *Reflect more.*
2. *Risk more.*
3. *Do more things that would live on after I die.*

I can hardly read those replies without feeling a bit nauseous. I know even those who live life all-out and expend themselves to their fullest potential for Christ might still wish that they would have done more. Joshua would be an example of such a person. He lived an amazing, victorious life like few others have ever known, and yet at the end of his life it was said, *Now Joshua was old and stricken in years; and the LORD said unto him, Thou art old and stricken in years, and there remaineth yet very much land to be possessed.* (Joshua 13:1) Right or wrong, as I look at the survey responses, I get the impression these were not likely men and women who did great things for God and only wish that they could have done more. No, I fear that these are part of the 10% crowd; those who live the entire length of their lives, but never come close to canvassing the breadth. These are among the many men and women whose lives were but a shell of what God had for them and left about 90% of His plan for their lives unfulfilled. A haunting saying comes to mind, *Unrelenting agony is the knowledge of opportunity lost; the place where the man I am comes face to face with the man I might have been.* The most sobering part is that by and large their race is run, and not much in the way of time or chance for any sort of mulligan. Writer Hunter S. Thompson pretty much summed up my thoughts exactly with these "petal to the medal" words.

> *Life should not be a journey to the grave with the intention of arriving safely in a pretty and well preserved body, but rather to skid in broadside in a cloud of smoke, thoroughly used up, totally worn out, and loudly proclaiming "Wow! What a Ride!"*[2]

An emerging way of sending out invitations to some scheduled event or celebration is no longer the standard, *RSVP,* but rather *REGRETS ONLY.* In other words, only respond to this invitation if you are unable to be in attendance. When it comes to the protocols of invitational etiquette, I am not for sure which is the more preferred, *RSVP* or *REGRETS ONLY;* but from the survey comments on the previous page, too many

---
❧

Will Borden lived his life with no regrets; while many of the rest of us wrestle from a life lived with only regrets.

---

people are coming to the end of their life with ONLY REGRETS. Will Borden lived his life with no regrets; while many of the rest of us wrestle from a life lived with only regrets. In light of this, the incredible harvest field God intended for us comes to naught. *The field is wasted, the land mourneth . . . Be ye ashamed . . . because the harvest of the field is perished.* (Joel 1:10-11)

Our next breath and all the God-facilitated opportunities that He introduces to us have a definite shelf-life. True, there is no expiration date stamped in ink-at least nothing visible; but make no mistake concerning the delicate and time-sensitive nature of the situation at hand. While God is timeless, ageless, and endless, His ushering in of opportunities your and my way is not. Be sure that you are a good steward of His opportunities before they (or you) expire.

*You pile up enough tomorrows, and you'll find
you've collected a lot of empty yesterdays.*
~Professor Harold Hill

*Between the great things we cannot do and the little things
we will not do, the danger is we shall do nothing*
~Anonymous

*Of all sad words of tongue or pen, the saddest
are these: It might have been.*
~John Greenleaf Whitier

*I have learned that if one advances confidently in the direction
of his dreams, and endeavors to live the life he has imagined,
he will meet with a success unexpected in common hours.*
~Henry David Thoreau

CHAPTER #10

A Final Appeal to Buy the Field

Buy my field, I pray thee. (Jeremiah 32:8)

BE FAMOUS

One of my favorite places to go for a meal when travelling out in California and other parts of the Southwest is a hamburger joint called, In-N-Out Burgers. I'm pretty much a burgers, fries and cherry pies kind of guy anyway, but the way these folks do it is simply amazing. Let me share with you why I love it there.

First of all, they incorporate scripture on their food product packaging. The Bible references are not necessarily printed in a prominent place (for their drink ware, it is on the inside lip of the bottom of the cup). Even so, I don't know of any other fast food chain with nearly three hundred stores which have the guts (or even the inclination) to do what they are doing.

But even more than that, what makes this establishment one of my very favorites is the food. The menu definitely takes its cue from the likes of Google's home page or the iPod family of products: simplified. There is a sum total of precisely one kind of french fries. They do not offer tater tots, curly fries, seasoned fries, waffle fries, or any other sort of cleverly devised spud combinations. If you are not pressed for time, you can even watch the potato go from its raw state to your plate before your very eyes, as all their fries are freshly cut and never frozen.

In that same spirit of simplification, there is a grand total of one sandwich on the menu, served three uncomplicated ways; the hamburger, the hamburger with cheese, (in some circles we would know this best as a cheeseburger) and the Double-Double. (yep, you guessed it; not one, but two hamburger patties) No grilled chicken, sliced ham, shaved beef, chicken fingers, foot long hotdogs, fish fillets, or mystery "rib" meat anywhere to be found.

While the Double-Double is the biggest sandwich they have officially listed on their unambiguous menu, I was eyewitness to a man that sashayed back to the table from the counter with tray in hand, and, in all honesty, what he was about to ingest looked like one of comic strip's Dagwood's towering sandwiches. I said to him, *Good night! That sandwich is fully loaded . . . exactly how many beef patties are in that puppy?* He responded sheepishly, *Six.* My eyes lit up. I was impressed, so I blurted, *I don't recall seeing that anywhere on the menu.* His lips puckered with a subtle, yet confident grin, demonstrating no sign of buyer's remorse. *They don't. You have to ask for it.* Wow, you simply have got to love a hamburger place like that!

In-N-Out locations haven't made their way to the Midwest, but we do have a retro hamburger place that is the next best thing. Steak n' Shake. A few years ago, the hamburger chain ran a catchy ad campaign complete with the slogan, *Steak n' Shake: Famous for Steakburgers.* And they have indeed become famous for that very thing. Months or even years before those commercials aired, perhaps some executives at the food chain gathered together for a boondoggle in some swanky destination spot. The agenda was uncomplicated and could be summed up as follows-What do we want to be when we grow up? That is to say, what do we want to be famous for?

Of course that corporate boardroom scenario is completely given to this author's conjecture, but rest assured that their brand positioning of *Famous for Steakburgers* was a highly intentional move and we can learn much from their purposefulness. What is it that you want your life to be famous for? Few of us will ever be in such a position of prominence that we are world famous, but we can be widely famous (well known) for something in the communities that we live. Most of us will never see our name engraved in a star on the Hollywood Walk of Fame. Nonetheless, we ought to strive to be men and women of renown in our schools, neighborhoods, church, places of work, and above all else, within the four walls of our own homes. And even if we live our days on earth in relative obscurity, we can be famous in the roll call of Heaven. If such were possible (and it is), what do we want to be famous for?

Famous appears ten times within the pages of scripture. Sometimes the people mentioned are famous for their great wickedness; other times for their great valor. Two mentions of famous are found in the Old Testament book of Ruth and the story of Boaz and Ruth woos' our thinking towards higher ground and inspires us to be known for a God honoring legacy which will endure the passing of time.

> *Then went Boaz up to the gate, and sat him down there: and, behold, the kinsman of whom Boaz spake came by; unto whom he said, Ho, such a one! turn aside, sit down here. And he turned aside, and sat down. And he took ten men of the elders of the city, and said, Sit ye down here. And they sat down. And he said unto the kinsman, Naomi, that is come again out of the country of Moab, selleth a parcel of land, which was our brother Elimelech's: And I thought to advertise thee, saying, Buy it before the inhabitants, and before the elders of my people. If thou wilt redeem it, redeem it: but if thou wilt not redeem it, then tell me, that I may know: for there is none to redeem it beside thee; and I am after thee. And he said, I will redeem it. Then said Boaz, What day thou buyest the field of the hand of Naomi, thou must buy it also of Ruth the Moabitess, the wife of the dead, to raise up the name of the dead upon his inheritance. And the kinsman said, I cannot redeem it for myself, lest I mar mine own inheritance:*

redeem thou my right to thyself; for I cannot redeem it. Now this was the manner in former time in Israel concerning redeeming and concerning changing, for to confirm all things; a man plucked off his shoe, and gave it to his neighbour: and this was a testimony in Israel. Therefore the kinsman said unto Boaz, Buy it for thee. So he drew off his shoe. And Boaz said unto the elders, and unto all the people, Ye are witnesses this day, that I have bought all that was Elimelech's, and all that was Chilion's and Mahlon's, of the hand of Naomi. Moreover Ruth the Moabitess, the wife of Mahlon, have I purchased to be my wife, to raise up the name of the dead upon his inheritance, that the name of the dead be not cut off from among his brethren, and from the gate of his place: ye are witnesses this day. And all the people that were in the gate, and the elders, said, We are witnesses. The LORD make the woman that is come into thine house like Rachel and like Leah, which two did build the house of Israel: and do thou worthily in Ephratah, and be famous in Bethlehem: (Ruth 4:1-11)

In these eleven monumental verses, we find the account of when Boaz took Ruth as his bride. But to do so, he had to first redeem her and purchase her field from the closest kinsman. The customary tradition of the day was that if a married man died and he and his yet living wife had no children, the eldest brother of the deceased was the next of kin. Along with that designation, came the responsibility to take his brother's widow and support the family. If the brother was unwilling or unable to redeem the widow, tradition dictated that either he (or the widow) would take off his shoe and give it to the next of kin. This gesture was symbolic of passing the baton of entitlement to the one whom he handed the shoe. By the way, if the widow was the one to pluck off his shoe, it was also customary that she would spit in the brother's face, as a testimony for his ignominy in not stepping up and fulfilling his obligations to her.

Of course, all of this is quite foreign to us today; in fact the whole process even seemed a bit dated during the time that this book was written. Verse seven describes this practice being the custom in *former times*. But what is noteworthy is that two disparate destinies were forever forged that day with the removal of the shoe from one man's foot and the placement of it into the hand of another. The line in the sand was drawn and the demarcation clear. One would go on to be famous, the other infamous. We'll revisit this climatic account in just a moment, so stay with me.

A POSITIVE SPIN ON ENTITLEMENT

Ours is a culture where an entitlement mentality seems increasingly pervasive. That is to say, there is a budding populous who feels as though they have the right to certain privileges. Many hold to a sense of entitlement whereby society in general and the government in particular, "owes" them a debt of gratitude or some such thing. Should this thinking persist, it is one of the social blights that has the capacity to unravel two-hundred plus years of socio-economic progress and will contribute to a loss of freedom in our nation. So understand that within the context of everyday usage in our culture today, the *It's my right* argument passes right through my ears like water through a sieve.

However, there is a more proper and biblical framework from which to view entitlement, and one of the places where it can be found is in the Old Testament book of Jeremiah.

And Jeremiah said, The word of the LORD came unto me, saying, Behold, Hanameel the son of Shallum thine uncle shall come unto thee, saying, Buy thee my field that is in Anathoth: for the right of redemption is thine to buy it. So Hanameel mine uncle's son came to me in the court of the prison according to the word of the LORD, and said unto me, Buy my field, I pray thee, that is in Anathoth, which is in the country of Benjamin: for the right of inheritance is thine, and the redemption is thine; buy it for thyself. Then I knew that this was the word of the LORD. And I bought the field of Hanameel my uncle's son, that was in Anathoth, and weighed him the money, even seventeen shekels of silver. (Jeremiah 32:6-9)

For anyone who is ready to step out in faith and buy the field, this Old Testament passage offers some final thoughts on doing exactly that. So let's parcel it down into smaller sections that we can more easily assimilate.

The Power to Buy the Field:

Buy thee my field that is in Anathoth: for the right of redemption is thine to buy it. (Verse 7b)

Although Jeremiah was imprisoned at the time, as first cousin he was still the nearest relative to Hanameel. In that culture, it was his responsibility and right to redeem the field and the first right of refusal to do so belonged to him as well.

This was no small matter as the future and livelihood of others hinged on his decision.

Similarly, Christians in a local church setting functioning as the body of Christ have been commissioned from God to go out into the field and impact our world. The responsibility is huge and the expectations are high. *For unto whomsoever much is given, of him shall be much required: and to whom men have committed much, of him they will ask the more.* (Luke 12:48) As sons of God (1 John 3:1) we have certain rights, and as ambassadors for Christ (2 Corinthians 5:20) we have been given much in the way of

---

With the blessings of sonship comes privileges, expectations, and, yes, being a child of God also includes obligations to buy the field.

---

responsibility from the One we represent. The right of redemption is ours, but when push comes to shove, we too often exercise our right of refusal and in effect declare, *Redeem thou my right to thyself; for I cannot redeem it.* (Ruth 4:6) With the blessings of sonship comes privileges, expectations, and, yes, being a child of God also includes obligations to buy the field.

The Plea to Buy the Field:
Buy my field, I pray thee. (Verse 8b)

Not only did Jeremiah have the authority or power to buy the field, but there was a heartfelt plea from the Owner for him to do so. For all who will give a listening ear, that same plea rings out today as God implores us to take action and to exercise our right to buy His field for us as well.

The Peace to Buy the Field:
Then I knew that this was the Word of the Lord. (Verse 8c)

The Lord had given Jeremiah a sign beforehand by telling him that Hanameel would come and ask him to buy his field. So when Hanameel did just that, Jeremiah knew this was a deal orchestrated in the heavens.

When buying the field in our own lives, there simply has to be *more of thee and less of me* in it, or stated more scripturally, *He must increase, but I must decrease.* (John 3:30) Be assured that once we commit to buy the field, trials and periods of testing will soon come our way and in such times if we do not know that we know that we know that we are following His will and not our own, odds are good we'll cave in and sell out. Like Jeremiah, we must know that the opportunity before us is from His hand and not brought about through our own posturing and scheming.

The Price to Buy to Buy the Field:

And I bought the field . . . and weighed him the money, even seventeen shekels of silver. (Verse 9a)

At first glance, the amount of seventeen shekels doesn't seem to be a very significant amount. Yet, the price paid in this transaction was noteworthy. First of all, as an imprisoned prophet, Jeremiah would be a man of very little means. Before he was placed into prison, the money he received as part of his priestly compensation would have been quite minimal. So seventeen shekels very well could have been the extent of his personal savings and net worth, and yet the God who owns everything required Jeremiah's all.

Sound at all familiar? (See chapter six) The Lord requires today our heart's all as well. While God uses the sacrificial giving today of His people to advance His causes on this earth, He is never after our money, but ever in loving pursuit of our heart. Such was the case with Jesus' response to the rich young ruler in Luke 18:22, *Now when Jesus heard these things, he said unto him, Yet lackest thou one thing: sell all that thou hast, and distribute unto the poor, and thou shalt have treasure in heaven: and come, follow me.* It has been my experience that when Christ has our heart, He will also have access to every other area in our life, including the checkbook.

Secondly, the exchange of money is also of note because Jeremiah is the next of kin. Upon Hanameel's death, the field in Anathoth would have simply been given to him for an inheritance as part of Hanameel's estate planning. Even so, the Lord was behind the transaction and required the exchange of money. Mind you, it was not an I.O.U. either, nor did Hanameel offer his cousin the convenience of a lay-away plan or some "six months same as cash" promotion. The terms were cash-on-delivery as Jeremiah weighed him the money on the spot.

There is a blight on dealings within Christendom today, namely that some Christians, especially those in full time service for the Lord such as myself, have an unbiblical expectation to be "exempt" from paying full price for things and are always on the lookout for some kind of a ministerial price break. I mean, the way some of us walk around the communities in which we live and serve, the old comic strip character, Sad Sack, would have nothing on us. As we go about our business affairs and dealings, it's almost as though our countenance and mannerisms places those around us on "Level Orange Alert," not for a terrorist threat, but for a moocher threat! I am very thankful for those who have the means and the heart to be an unexpected blessing to those in full-time ministry, but God forbid that we should ever plummet to the pitiful mental state where we expect such generosity and preferential treatment.

I don't fully understand why God required Jeremiah's all, particularly when he was next in line to receive the field as his inheritance. But this account is another reminder of the steep price tag which swings suspended from God's will for every life. If it helps lessen the sticker shock and make the purchase price more palatable, I would remind you that there is a far steeper cost incurred for NOT buying the field. The cost of disobedience is painfully high and who of us is able to assign a price to regret?

A third reason, and the one most curious behind this transaction, is that Jeremiah knew that in the near future, all the land (including the land he was buying) would be laid to ruin and taken over by the Chaldeans. In the first five verses of this chapter the Lord reveals to the prophet how all of Judah will fall and be overrun. Then in verses six thru nine He instructs Jeremiah to buy the field anyway. This instruction has to be just about the most unusual and oddly timed investment counsel ever given for all time! To our way of thinking, this would sure seem like a most opportune time to sell, not to buy, and at MSRP no less.

Need we to be reminded that He is God and we are not. Scripture is replete with unconventional instructions from God that we could not possibly understand from our limited line of sight. So, if God places some "out-of-the-box" thinking on our hearts, we would be wise to put conventional wisdom on the shelf and simply do the work He has assigned us to do.

The One Who Would Become Infamous:

Let's revisit our earlier account in the book of Ruth, where two disparate legacies were forged that fateful day. A group of ten men were called together at the gates of the city to witness a real estate transaction between two kinfolk. But the writer of scripture thought it necessary only to honor one of those men by sharing with us his name. *Then went Boaz up to the gate, and sat him down there: and, behold, the kinsman of whom Boaz spake came by; unto whom he said, Ho, such a one! turn aside, sit down here. And he turned aside, and sat down.* (Ruth 4:1) Boaz was the one who was mentioned, but throughout the corridors of time, the other man will forever remain nameless. Not because he was a private man of discretion who preferred anonymity and to live in the shadows of public notoriety, but rather because his name was not worthy of an honorable mentioning.

Actually, if we dig a little deeper, perhaps we would deduce that his name is subliminally encrypted in the very first verse; possibly his full legal name was, *Such A. One!* We are privy to only the first name of every other character within the whole realm of scripture, but with this individual, we have not only the first and last names, but his middle initial as well! The point is that he obviously had a name, but because he shrank from the call of duty, it will never be known beyond his immediate family and those ten men of the city. As such, he will never be famous but rather has become infamous; that is notorious for his time in the spotlight where he walked away and left a good, right, and honorary deed undone.

Look at the first four verses again of Ruth 4, for in it we see that Boaz tells him, *Naomi . . . selleth a parcel of land . . . If thou wilt redeem it, redeem it.* Which Mr. One promptly replied, *I will redeem it.* Case closed. Roger that. Who's up for getting some pizza? Not just yet, because in the spirit of full disclosure, Boaz then proceeded to read the legalese at the bottom of the contract in four-point font. *Then said Boaz, What day thou buyest the field of the hand of Naomi, thou must buy it also of Ruth the Moabitess, the wife of the dead, to raise up the name of the dead upon his inheritance.* (Ruth 4:5) Boaz reveals to him that it is not just a nice tract of land to add to the investment portfolio, but whoever gets the parcel of land also gets the young widow. For most men, this would be a welcomed bonus, a delightful two-for-one kind of deal. Only one problem. There was already a wife and kids at home with a wedding album displayed on the coffee table, and photos of the Mediterranean cruise they took on their honeymoon proudly lining the hallway wall. Nope, this deal would not bode well at all with Mrs. One. I mean, what would the new girl be called around the house, Mrs. Two?

To thicken the plot and make an already tense situation even more so, any children that would come of this union would need to be written into the will, carving out more pieces from the same inheritance pie and diminishing what his current children would receive. With this "catch" coming to light, he pulls back from his earlier expression of enthusiasm, looks red-faced down at the ground as he shuffles his feet in the dirt and nervously mumbles, *I cannot redeem it for myself, lest I mar mine own inheritance: redeem thou my right to thyself for I cannot redeem it.* (Ruth 4:6) Twice he muttered, *I cannot redeem it,* because "I cannot" has a more noble, less condemning ring to it than "I will not."

And so, in the most unsuspecting of moments, and for the time span of a blink of an eye, Such A. One comes to the intersection of destiny and decision and of all things, locks the brakes up and does a U-ey, driving off in the opposite direction as he fades away into an inglorious sunset. Case and window of opportunity closed. Forever.

Customs and protocols have changed a lot since then for certain, but one thing has not. Buying the field always comes at a personally high price. When it comes to leaving a legacy to the generations that follow us, most Christians have made their peace with being remembered only as "John Doe", the imperceptible contemporary equivalent to "Such A. One."

The One Who Would Become Famous:

While one nameless man sealed his fate that day by refusing to buy the field, Boaz secured his legacy by purchasing it. He wasn't the most likely of men to buy the field and redeem Ruth, but he was the most loyal. He probably wasn't the most winsome, but he was the one most willing. He wasn't the closest of kin, but he was the most considerate. And his story of redemption, which is a foreshadowing of the Lord Jesus Christ's redemptive work on Calvary, is told the world over today. He and Ruth are famous for the events of that fateful day and the lineage that would come from their union. They would have a son together named Obed, who would have a son named Jesse, who would in turn have a son named, David. King David. And now you know, as Radio Commentator Paul Harvey once coined, *The Rest of the Story*. All of this birthed from one man's unexpected resolve, in the unlikeliest of settings, and in the most unsuspecting of moments, to buy the field.

EPILOGUE

The Rest Of *Your* Story

or the last ten chapters, we have been informed that we have a field, and that God's field for us is sacred. As such we must consider, buy, work, pay for, and stay in the field, come what may. The story of those who did man up and buy the field and stayed working in it are forever sealed, as are the accounts of those who did not. Our Alpha and Omega God, Who sees the beginning from the end, (Revelation 1:8) has the knowledge that, *all our days are passed away in thy wrath: we spend our years as a tale that is told.* (Psalm 90:9) In other words, in His omniscience, God knows how our story will end, but no one else does, including you. As a help, so that the rest of your story will be about following His will for your life, I offer this closing allegory.

> In the solitude of a deep, nighttime slumber, I had a sweet dream; at least I believed it was only such. It was a dream in which I was kneeling before the throne of grace, as I heard softly whispered to me, *Let thine eyes be on the field.* Not entirely certain what it was that was said, I continued to bow in silent reverence, listening still, and soon the inaudible voice whispered gently again, *Lift up your eyes, and look on the fields.* Confident this time of the words that I heard, but uncertain of what to do next, by the Holy Spirit *I was moved . . . to ask*

of [my] *father a field,* as I cried out to Him, *What shall I do, Lord?* It pleased Him to open my eyes and to reveal more of His will for me, as I then carefully *considereth a field.* I counted the costs, mindful that *fields shall be bought with money,* and abruptly came to the conclusion that *I cannot redeem it.* As soon as such thoughts had crept through the entrance door of my mind, His reassuring answer was, *Buy thee my field: for the right of redemption is thine to buy it.* My will stiffened as I refused to yield, hesitant to obey His voice and leading. I looked about and glanced at the fine fields of others around me; they appeared much more fitting and far more to be desired. His reply, unlike my delay, was prompt. *Neither shalt thou covet thy neighbour's field. Go not to glean in another field, neither go from hence, but abide here.* I cried aloud, but your field for me is a lowly, out of the way field of such insignificance. Just as swiftly and more sternly His words to me were, "No. For my *field . . . shall be holy unto the LORD.*"

Anxious thoughts of failure, uncertainty, and what I must leave behind consumed me as I inquired, "What if *the fields shall yield no meat?*" But even as the words flowed from my tongue, I knew that come what may, I *should rejoice in the LORD, I will joy in the God of my salvation.* My hesitancy lingered at the decision before me. My loving Father is ever patient and kind but firmly reminded me that the longer I hesitate, the greater my procrastination, then the more *the field is wasted,* and *the land mourneth; because the harvest of the field is perished.* Time was short. The opportunity was fleeting. The appointed hour had all but passed.

Amidst the tranquil silence, one more statement was whispered, more softly even than the first. One last petition, while there was still time. One final plea before it was too late and all would be lost. *Buy my field, I pray thee.* I could delay no longer. The patient love from which those words came chipped away at my self-centered, unworthy excuses, as I at long last boldly and loudly exclaimed, *I will redeem it . . . and for joy thereof goeth and selleth all that* [I] *hath, and buyeth that field.* Without communicating any gestures of guilt for my trifling and delay, my Father said, *Come, my beloved, let us go forth into the field.* And from that point on, if any onlookers were ever asked what became of me, and where did my Father go, as a memorial to His grace it was said, *And they went out both of them into the field.*

About the Author

ob Fleshman and his wife, Michelle, have been married for more than 20 years and have four children: Tanner, Krista, Kaylee, and Kylie. The Fleshman's make their home in Unionville, MO, where Rob is the Pastor of Midway Baptist Church.

RESOURCES

Buy the Field University

As a help to like-minded independent Baptist churches, Pastors, Bible Colleges, Christian camps and other organizations, we are pleased to announce, *Buy the Field University*. This challenging, soul-stirring forum for Christians is where the author will come to your church and personally help encourage God's people to buy the field God has for them. Our time together at *Buy the Field University* is divided up into three distinct teaching sessions:

Module 1:   *Find God's Call for Your Life*
Module 2:   *Follow God's Call for Your Life*
Module 3:   *Finish God's Call for Your Life*

While this inspirational venue can be customized to meet local churches specific scheduling needs, we have seen it fit well into a format where Module 1 is covered on Friday evening and Modules 2 & 3 are taught on Saturday morning.

<u>Pastors & other ministry leaders:</u> To bring *Buy the Field University* to your church, connect with us via one of the means on the following page. We would love to hear from you and strive to be of help to your ministry in any way possible!

Connect via Social Media

facebook.com/mymidway.org
facebook.com/rob.fleshman
twitter.com/robfleshman
brofleshman@gmail.com

Connect via U.S. Mail

Pastor Rob Fleshman
Midway Baptist Church
P.O. Box 33
Unionville, MO 63565
660.947.3087

REFERENCES

Chapter 1

1. Samuel Butler. His translation of, *Odyssey IX*
   http://classics.mit.edu/Homer/odyssey.html

Chapter 2

1. *Our Daily Bread*, September 5, 1984
2. H.A. Ironside. *Illustrations of Bible Truth.* Moody Press, 1945. 37-39.

Chapter 3

1. *Practical Bible Illustrations from Yesterday and Today.* AMG International, INC. 1996. Electronic Edition STEP Files Copyright 2005, QuickVerse.
2. John Bunyan. *The Pilgrim's Progress.* London, 1678. 246-249

Chapter 6

1. Mark Hamby. His republication of Charles Hadden Spurgeon's, *John Ploughman's Talk.* Lamplighter Publishing, a division of Cornerstone Family Ministries, Inc. 2006, 9

2. ibid, 11-12.
3. ibid, 13.

Chapter 7

1. Kristi Umbreit. *Associated Press, AP News Archive* May 21, 1990. Last accessed on November 14, 2012. http://www.apnewsarchive. com/1990/Woman-Runs-Marathon-by-Mistake/id 93316d331c b21a97b534b9426a957222

2. Indian Peaks Wilderness Association (IPWA) website. Last accessed on November 14, 2012. http://www.indianpeakswilderness.org/IPWA_news_4_01b.htm

Chapter 8

1. Eustace Carey, Francis Wayland, Jeremiah Chaplain, William Carey. *Memoir of William Carey, D.D.: Late Missionary to Bengal; Professor of Oriental Languages in the College of Fort William, Calculta.* London. Jackson and Walford (Google eBook)
2. Jonathan Going, J.F. Schroeder, J.M Cress. *The Christian Library: A Weekly Republication of Popular Religious Works,* Volume 8. New York. (Google eBook)
3. Lucas Morel. Compiled this comparison from the Chronology in *Selected Speeches and Writings/ Lincoln* by Don E. Fehrenbacher, ed., 1992. Last accessed on April 7, 2013. http://www.abrahamlincolnonline.org/lincoln/education/ failures.htm
4. George Stover, Jr. *Integrity: The Last Great Battle.* Xulon Press, 2012.
5. Allistair Begg. His updated edit and revision of Charles Hadden Spurgeon's original devotional, *Morning & Evening.* Crossway, 2003.

Chapter 9

1. John Steinbeck. *Cannery Row.* Penguin Books; Centennial Edition, 2002.
2. Anthony Campolo. *Who Switched the Price Tags,* Word Publishing, 1986.

CPSIA information can be obtained at www.ICGtesting.com
Printed in the USA
LVOW12s0324020814

397122LV00004B/5/P